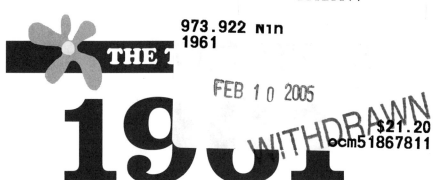

## Other books in the
## Turbulent 60s series:

# THE TURBULENT 60s

# 1961

James Haley, *Book Editor*

Bonnie Szumski, *Publisher*
Scott Barbour, *Managing Editor*
David M. Haugen, *Series Editor*

GREENHAVEN
PRESS®

THOMSON

™

GALE

San Diego • Detroit • New York • San Francisco • Cleveland
New Haven, Conn. • Waterville, Maine • London • Munich

Cover credit: © Associated Press/AP
John F. Kennedy Library, 12, 22, 75
Library of Congress, 60, 109
National Archives, 95

LIBRARY OF CONGRESS CATALOGING-IN-PUBLICATION DATA

1961 / James Haley, book editor.
    p. cm. — (The turbulent 60s)
Includes bibliographical references and index.
ISBN 0-7377-1504-9 (lib. : alk. paper) — ISBN 0-7377-1505-7 (pbk. : alk. paper)
    1. United States—History—1961–1969—Sources. 2. Nineteen sixty-one, A.D.—
Sources. 3. History, Modern—1945–1989—Sources. I. Haley, James, 1968– .
II. Series.
E841.A13 2004
973.922—dc21
                                                                            2003044811

# CONTENTS

space flight aboard *Freedom 7*, an important milestone for the nation's space program.

Berlin Wall, which would stand as a symbol of Cold War animosities until its fall in 1989.

tracted hundreds of protesters and resulted in
mass arrests.

# FOREWORD

The 1960s were a period of immense change in America. What many view as the complacency of the 1950s gave way to increased radicalism in the 1960s. The newfound activism of America's youth turned an entire generation against the social conventions of their parents. The rebellious spirit that marked young adulthood was no longer a stigma of the outcast but rather a badge of honor among those who wanted to remake the world. And in the 1960s, there was much to rebel against in America. The nation's involvement in Vietnam was one of the catalysts that helped galvanize young people in the early 1960s. Another factor was the day-to-day Cold War paranoia that seemed to be the unwelcome legacy of the last generation. And for black Americans in particular, there was the inertia of the civil rights movement that, despite seminal victories in the 1950s, had not effectively countered the racism still plaguing the country. All of these concerns prompted the young to speak out, to decry the state of the nation that would be their inheritance.

The 1960s, then, may best be remembered for its spirit of confrontation. The student movement questioned American imperialism, militant civil rights activists confronted their elders over the slow progress of change, and the flower children faced the nation's capitalistic greed and conservative ethics and opted to create a counterculture. There was a sense of immediacy to all this activism, and people put their bodies on the line to bring about change. Although there were reactionaries and conservative holdouts, the general feeling was that a united spirit of resistance could stop the inevitability of history. People could shape their own destinies, and together they could make a better world. As sixties chronicler Todd Gitlin writes, "In the Sixties it seemed especially true that History with a capital H had come down to earth, either interfering with life or making it possible: and that within History, or threaded through it, people were living with a supercharged density: lives were bound up with one another, making claims on one another, drawing one another into the common project."

Perhaps not everyone experienced what Gitlin describes, but few would argue that the nation as a whole was left untouched by the radical notions of the times. The women's movement, the civil rights movement, and the antiwar movement left indelible marks. Even the hippie movement left behind a relaxed morality and a more ecological mindset. Popular culture, in turn, reflected these changes: Music became more diverse and experimental, movies adopted more adult themes, and fashion attempted to replicate the spirit of uninhibited youth. It seemed that every facet of American culture was affected by the pervasiveness of revolution in the 1960s, and despite the diversity of rebellions, there remained a sense that all were related to, as Gitlin puts it, "the common project."

Of course, this communal zeitgeist of the 1960s is best attributed to the decade in retrospect. The 1960s were not a singular phenomenon but a progress of individual days, of individual years. Greenhaven Press follows this rubric in The Turbulent Sixties series. Each volume of this series is devoted to the major events that define a specific year of the decade. The events are discussed in carefully chosen articles. Some of these articles are written by historians who have the benefit of hindsight, but most are contemporary accounts that reveal the complexity, confusion, excitement, and turbulence of the times. Each article is prefaced by an introduction that places the event in its historical context. Every anthology is also introduced by an essay that gives shape to the entire year. In addition, the volumes in the series contain time lines, each of which gives an at-a-glance structure to the major events of the topic year. A bibliography of helpful sources is also provided in each anthology to offer avenues for further study. With these tools, readers will better understand the developments in the political arena, the civil rights movement, the counterculture, and other facets of American society in each year. And by following the trends and events that define the individual years, readers will appreciate the revolutionary currents of this tumultuous decade—the turbulent sixties.

# The Year of Optimism

The year 1961 ushered in an era of sweeping political and social change in the United States and roused Americans out of the civic passivity that had predominated throughout much of the 1950s. It was a year in which the nation's security and future were continually threatened by escalating Cold War tensions with the Soviet Union. Moral standards also shifted as a vocal minority of middle-class Americans felt compelled to end the shameful treatment of black Americans in the South, who were still being denied basic rights of citizenship nearly one hundred years after the abolition of slavery. Many of the issues that would come to characterize the turbulence of the later years of the 1960s—the struggle for civil rights, America's role in developing nations, the Vietnam War, and the student protest movement—fell into place during 1961. The key quality of 1961, however, was a renewed sense of idealism. After a decade of unquestioning faith in the status quo, 1961 found growing pockets of Americans anxious to move the nation toward its unfulfilled promise as the world's exemplar of freedom and equality and confident that such promise could be achieved.

## A New President Encourages a Global Outlook

One catalyst for change in the months ahead was set in motion by the results of the November 1960 presidential election. Forty-three-year-old John F. Kennedy had defeated Republican challenger Richard M. Nixon by a slim margin of just 112,881 votes out of a total of 68,838,565 votes cast. While the narrow victory was not a mandate for Kennedy's "New Frontier," the platform of pragmatic liberalism that he had outlined during the campaign, it indicated that the majority were looking to break away from President Dwight D. Eisenhower's administration, in which Nixon had served as vice president. An elderly conservative and World War II general, Eisenhower had played a grandfatherly role for the nation during his two terms in office, presiding over a decade remembered mainly for its bland conformity. The Kennedy camp regarded him as having long since run out of fresh ideas and had campaigned with the slogan "Let's Get This Country Moving Again," a not-so-subtle reminder of Eisenhower's senescence and the ongoing economic recession that had resulted in high unemployment in the 1960s.

In the weeks leading up to his inauguration, Kennedy's popularity grew as the public became better acquainted with its new leader. The youthful president-elect showed himself to be full of the energy and can-do optimism that had been lacking in his aging predecessor. Appealing to the public's penchant for both tradition and glamour, Kennedy's beautiful wife and two young children generated excitement and pride for the new First Fam-

*Americans were excited to have a young, energetic president and his family in the White House.*

ily. Many observers were also reassured by the sound judgment Kennedy displayed in selecting his administration officials. These aides were culled from the elite ranks of the so-called Eastern Establishment—Harvard intellectuals, Wall Street lawyers and financiers, and the chief executives of powerful corporations. As journalist David Halberstam observes in his book *The Best and the Brightest*, Kennedy's administration would carry "a sense that the best men had been summoned forth from the country to [bring] . . . a new, strong, dynamic spirit to our historic role in world affairs, not necessarily to bring the American dream to reality here at home, but to bring it to reality elsewhere in the world."[1]

Accordingly, on January 20, 1961, in Washington, D.C., President Kennedy delivered an inaugural address that strongly advocated a global role for America's democratic values. In the president's view, freedom and democracy were under assault in poor nations emerging from years of colonial rule, due in large measure to the growing spread of Soviet-backed communism. He challenged a new generation of Americans, as heirs of the American Revolution, to live up to their duty to defend the human rights and freedom of peoples both at home and abroad. Imploring the public to help those "struggling to break the bonds of mass misery," the president famously stated, "Ask not what your country can do for you; ask what you can do for your country."[2] Kennedy's address served as more than romantic bluster against the spread of communism—it inspired many people, particularly the young, to take a more activist role in their own country and the world. The call was not aimed at sparking war-hawk patriotism but at maintaining that the American ideals of freedom, democracy, justice, and equality were worth struggling for.

## The Peace Corps Attracts Young Volunteers

Young people anxious to follow the president's advice and serve their country in a humanitarian capacity abroad found an exciting new opportunity in the Peace Corps. This volunteer organization was created by Kennedy on March 1, 1961, through an executive order. According to the president, the Peace Corps would recruit volunteers with special skills and place them in leadership roles in impoverished nations, helping to "build growing and independent nations where men can live in dignity, liberated from the bonds of hunger, ignorance and poverty." The volunteers would accomplish this mission by working as educators, scientists, public health administrators, and engineers in "the villages, the mountains, the towns and the factories of dozens of struggling nations."[3]

The president's plan for a pilot program to train two thousand overseas workers was an immediate hit on many college campuses across the country, where the current generation of students had shown increasing concern for issues of social justice. Early recruitment drives at eastern universities were packed with eager volunteers. Some observers, however, questioned whether the enthusiasm of pampered middle-class Americans would survive the challenge of adjusting to the food, culture, disease, and general deprivation of the Third World. As a condition of service in the Peace Corps, volunteers would be required to live "under primitive conditions . . . simply and unostentatiously among the people they have come to assist."[4] In May 1961 Indiana University professor George H.T. Kimble raised these questions in a *New York Times Magazine* article:

> Consider, first, the physical problems. These run the gamut from keeping comfortable to keeping alive. The Congo [African nation], for instance, is no place like Connecticut or California. . . . Its staple foods . . . lack variety and are deficient in protein and other necessary ingredients of a healthy diet. . . . He is a lucky Congolese who . . . has not had malaria, . . . dysentery, typhoid or paratyphoid, and one or more worm infections.[5]

A minority of liberals and conservatives alike also distrusted the stated purpose of the Peace Corps, regarding its putative humanitarian goals as mere U.S. propaganda and a smokescreen for limiting the rise of communism in developing nations. Kimble was not alone in arguing that the Peace Corps would be the "target of every political sharpshooter at home and abroad . . . [and] is already being called an arm of American diplomacy, a weapon with which to fight the cold war, and a front organization for the CIA."[6]

Undeterred by questions of physical comfort and politics, large numbers of young Americans continued to express an interest in putting their post-college careers on hold and working for peace and prosperity in poor nations. In September 1961 journalist Benjamin DeMott asserted in *Harper's* magazine that "There are no signs yet that these voices of doubt have caused any drop in public interest in the young volunteers. . . . The volunteers I talked to at Rutgers [University] were uncommonly winning young men, shrewd, clearheaded, and admirably diverse in abilities."[7]

## Fighting for Civil Rights at Home

While the Peace Corps satisfied a quest to advance American ideals abroad, it also caused some Americans to ask whether the United States truly practiced the noble values it was now so eager to inculcate in foreign peoples. Journalist George E. Sokolsky wondered, "Is the United States 'the land of the free and the home of the brave'? Precisely how does that work out in practice? . . . The honest [Peace Corps volunteer] will be stumped. He cannot answer these questions without many modifications."[8] Sokolsky's comment concurred with the opinion of other whites, who were increasingly ashamed of the injustices perpetrated against black Americans in the southern United States. In 1961 blacks in many parts of the South were still denied the right to vote, the right to travel freely between states and avail themselves of basic services along the way, and the right to attend desegregated schools, despite recent Supreme Court decisions guaranteeing these rights.

In 1955 the Reverend Martin Luther King Jr. had led blacks in Montgomery, Alabama, on a year-long boycott of the city's public buses. The successful protest brought an end to the segregation of black passengers, who, prior to the boycott, had been confined to seats in the rear of buses. Two years later, in 1957, King formed the Southern Christian Leadership Conference (SCLC) with other black religious leaders in order to enlarge the battle against segregation in the South. Throughout 1961 the SCLC led voter registration drives and organized large-scale demonstrations against restaurants, public transportation carriers, hotels, and other businesses that continued to deny blacks service or enforce segregation against them. King was an inspirational figure, blessed with great powers of oratory, who modeled his nonviolent protests on the example of Mohandas Gandhi, an Indian leader who had advocated civil disobedience in the struggle for India's independence from Britain.

Encouraged by King's example, groups of black college students in the South began to organize sit-ins and demonstrations of their own. In 1961, after interviewing black activists at Virginia Union College for *Harper's* magazine, reporter Charlotte Devree was struck by their commitment. Observed Devree, "They were on fire with their purpose. . . . It seemed to me that their truly desperate struggle—the beatings, the reprisals, the jailing—was rewarding them with the very identity and pride that Negroes in the United States have so long sought in vain. This is already their secret triumph." In addition, she noted that white students were getting involved in the civil rights movement beyond mere lip service. According to a black student interviewed by Devree, "Whites had written from campuses North and South . . . to ask how they could help. He'd already been to a secret meeting organized in a Southern city—over a hundred white and Negro students had come, from all over the country."[9]

Although whites had participated in the civil rights struggle prior to 1961—King had the support of prominent white activists in the North—the involvement of middle-class college kids was a striking development. It spoke to a growing tide of activism rolling through American campuses—a new willingness to do something about the racism their parents had turned a blind eye to for too long. In September 1961 King maintained that the black students' example had stirred young whites to join the burgeoning movement for social justice. He credited black college students with "taking our whole nation back to those great wells of democracy which were dug deep by the Founding Fathers in the formulation of the Constitution and the Declaration of Independence."[10]

## Freedom Riders Are Attacked

On May 4, 1961, several whites experienced firsthand the indignities routinely suffered by black bus travelers in the South. A group of thirteen protesters, consisting of seven blacks and six whites, left Washington, D.C., on a series of "Freedom Rides." Organized by the New York–based Congress of Racial Equality, an interracial civil rights association, the plan was for the protesters to ride Greyhound buses into the Deep South, challenging the segregation of black passengers in buses and bus terminals. Racial segregation in interstate carriers had been banned by the U.S. Interstate Commerce Commission in 1955, and a 1960 Supreme Court ruling had declared segregation in bus and train terminals unconstitutional. Nevertheless, several southern jurisdictions were blatantly ignoring federal law.

Outside Anniston, Alabama, one of the Freedom Riders' buses was firebombed, and the frightened passengers were beaten bloody by a white mob as they fled the bus. A second bus was

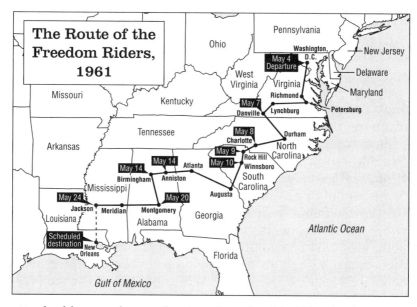

The Route of the Freedom Riders, 1961

attacked by another mob when it arrived in Birmingham, Alabama. Several days later, a separate group of Freedom Riders, who had joined the protest from Nashville, was attacked in Montgomery, Alabama. In this instance, Attorney General Robert Kennedy had received assurances from local authorities that police protection would be provided, though none was forthcoming. Kennedy administration representative John Seigenthaler, sent to Montgomery to do his best to ensure the riders' safety, was beaten unconscious as he attempted to protect a black child from the mob's onslaught.

The Freedom Rides received widespread media coverage and brought further attention to the intransigent racism that afflicted a large section of the country. Most important, the rides confirmed the commitment of many participants to the civil rights struggle. White college student Robert Martinson, who, in June 1961 had traveled from California to Jackson, Mississippi, to participate in the rides, remarked that the "Riders have shown the entire nation the depth of their attachment to freedom and democracy."[11]

Not all observers of the Freedom Rides, both within and outside the civil rights movement, shared Martinson's opinion of the protests. In a year that found American ideals exported overseas with the Peace Corps, the Freedom Rides engendered a debate over how racial equality could best be brought to America's own backyard. On May 24, 1961, Attorney General Robert Kennedy had urged the Freedom Riders to enter a "cooling-off" period to preclude further violence, asserting that the courts, not the streets, were the preferred venue for enforcing federal civil rights law in the Deep South. Civil rights activists, including Martin Luther King Jr., rejected this plea, and the Freedom Rides continued throughout the summer and into the fall, resulting in mass demonstrations and arrests by mid-December. According to Bruce Miroff in his book *Pragmatic Illusions: The Presidential Politics of John F. Kennedy*, "A Gallup poll in late June showed 63 percent of those questioned disapproving of the rides." Reflecting the public's disapproval, Miroff describes Kennedy's public statements on the protesters as offering half-hearted support, "as if the freedom riders were a highly unpopular group of dissidents whose rights had to be protected despite the group's obnoxious nature."[12] Kennedy's reluctance to endorse the Freedom Riders pointed to a deepening divide between the majority of Americans, who seemed to favor more gradual change, and the upstart coalition of radical young blacks and whites anxious to bring the South into the twentieth century. This generational divide would prove to be a significant factor in the later years of the 1960s, when frustrated young blacks turned to the separatism of the black nationalist movement and the militancy of the Black Panthers to achieve their goals.

## Optimism Amidst International Unrest

Throughout 1961 the nation's growing domestic turbulence was largely overshadowed by rising Cold War animosities and the looming threat of nuclear war with the Soviet Union. From the failed invasion of Cuba at the Bay of Pigs to the rise of the Berlin Wall to the spread of communism in Southeast Asia, President Kennedy dealt with one Cold War crisis after another with results that inevitably antagonized Soviet premier Nikita S. Khrushchev. Americans were reminded of the very real possibility of nuclear annihilation in several of Kennedy's addresses during the summer and fall of 1961. A few families even heeded the president's calls for private fallout shelters and built backyard bunkers under the mistaken belief that materials from the local hardware store could protect them against a nuclear attack. Yet after a decade of withdrawal into prosperous suburban communities, the majority of Americans seemed largely unaffected by the atmosphere of international crisis as the year drew to a close. This sense of optimism and invulnerability would soon be shattered by the assassination of President Kennedy in 1963 and America's full-scale involvement in the Vietnam War. And by the mid-1960s, the small numbers of young people who had taken up the cause of social justice in 1961 would stand at the vanguard of a formidable antiwar movement. The rapid-fire events of 1961, both at home and abroad, pulled the nation inexorably into the new decade by laying the groundwork for the change to come.

## Notes

1. David Halberstam, *The Best and the Brightest.* New York: Random House, 1972, p. 41.

2. Quoted in John W. Gardner, ed., *To Turn the Tide.* New York: Harper & Brothers, 1962, pp. 7, 10.

3. Quoted in Gardner, *To Turn the Tide*, pp. 157–59.

4. Quoted in Gardner, *To Turn the Tide*, p. 159.

5. George H.T. Kimble, "Challenges to the Peace Corps," *New York Times Magazine*, May 14, 1961, p. 98.

6. Kimble, "Challenges to the Peace Corps," p. 99.

7. Benjamin DeMott, "The Peace Corps' Secret Mission," *Harper's*, September 1961, pp. 63–64.

8. George E. Sokolsky, "Can the Peace Corps Do the Job?" *Saturday Review*, June 17, 1961, p. 18.

9. Charlotte Devree, "The Young Negro Rebels," *Harper's*, October 1961, pp. 133–34.

10. Martin Luther King Jr., "The Time for Freedom Has Come," *New York Times Magazine*, September 3, 1961, p. 119.

11. Robert Martinson, "Prison Notes of a Freedom Rider," *Nation*, January 6, 1962, p. 6.

12. Bruce Miroff, *Pragmatic Illusions: The Presidential Politics of John F. Kennedy.* New York: David McKay, 1976, p. 236.

## ARTICLE 1

# In Defense of Freedom: President Kennedy's Inaugural Address

**By John F. Kennedy**

In the fall of 1960, forty-three-year-old senator John F. Kennedy, a Massachusetts Democrat, narrowly defeated his Republican challenger, Vice President Richard Nixon, and was elected the thirty-fifth president of the United States. The young president entered office at a time when the Cold War struggle against the Soviet Union had grown increasingly forbidding. Just days before Kennedy's inauguration, Soviet premier Nikita Khrushchev had asserted that the Soviet Union would win the Cold War through "national liberation wars" in Asia, Africa, and Latin America, which would replace colonialist governments with Communist regimes. Some observers maintained that Kennedy's predecessor, two-term conservative President Dwight D. Eisenhower, had not spent enough on the nation's defense program. As a result, a nuclear "missile gap" had arisen between the United States and the well-armed Soviet Union, which was showing brazen support for Communist takeovers in developing nations.

In the following inaugural address delivered on January 20, 1961, in Washington, D.C., President Kennedy rises to Khrushchev's challenge by asserting that the defeat of Communist aggression around the world

John F. Kennedy, Inaugural Address, January 20, 1961.

will be a top priority of his administration. To achieve this goal, he asks the American people to accept responsibility for the defense of democracy and freedom wherever it may be threatened. Kennedy served as president until November 22, 1963, when he was assassinated in Dallas, Texas.

**W**e observe today not a victory of a party but a celebration of freedom—symbolizing an end as well as a beginning—signifying renewal as well as change. For I have sworn before you and Almighty God the same solemn oath our forebears prescribed nearly a century and three quarters ago.

The world is very different now. For man holds in his mortal hands the power to abolish all forms of human poverty and all forms of human life. And yet the same revolutionary beliefs for which our forebears fought are still at issue around the globe—the belief that the rights of man come not from the generosity of the state but from the hand of God.

We dare not forget today that we are the heirs of that first revolution. Let the word go forth from this time and place, to friend and foe alike, that the torch has been passed to a new generation of Americans—born in this century, tempered by war, disciplined by a hard and bitter peace, proud of our ancient heritage—and unwilling to witness or permit the slow undoing of those human rights to which this Nation has always been committed, and to which we are committed today at home and around the world.

Let every nation know, whether it wishes us well or ill, that we shall pay any price, bear any burden, meet any hardship, support any friend, oppose any foe to assure the survival and success of liberty.

## Aiding Friends

This much we pledge—and more.

To those old allies whose cultural and spiritual origins we share, we pledge the loyalty of faithful friends. United, there is little we cannot do in a host of cooperative ventures. Divided, there is little we can do—for we dare not meet a powerful challenge at odds and split asunder.

To those new states whom we welcome to the ranks of the free, we pledge our word that one form of colonial control shall not have passed away merely to be replaced by a far more iron tyranny. We shall not always expect to find them supporting our view. But we shall always hope to find them strongly supporting their own freedom—and to remember that, in the past, those who foolishly sought power by riding the back of the tiger ended up inside.

To those peoples in the huts and villages of half the globe struggling to break the bonds of mass misery, we pledge our best efforts to help them help themselves, for whatever period is required—not because the Communists may be doing it, not because we seek their votes, but because it is right. If a free society cannot help the many who are poor, it cannot save the few who are rich.

To our sister republics south of our border, we offer a special pledge—to convert our good words into good deeds—in a new alliance for progress—to assist free men and free governments in casting off the chains of poverty. But this peaceful revolution of hope cannot become the prey of hostile powers. Let all our neighbors know that we shall join with them to oppose aggression or subversion anywhere in the Americas. And let every other

*John Fitzgerald Kennedy is sworn in as the thirty-fifth president of the United States on January 20, 1961.*

power know that this hemisphere intends to remain the master of its own house.

To that world assembly of sovereign states, the United Nations, our last best hope in an age where the instruments of war have far outpaced the instruments of peace, we renew our pledge of support—to prevent it from becoming merely a forum for invective—to strengthen its shield of the new and the weak—and to enlarge the area in which its writ may run.

## Opposing Aggressive Adversaries

Finally, to those nations who would make themselves our adversary, we offer not a pledge but a request: that both sides begin anew the quest for peace, before the dark powers of destruction unleashed by science engulf all humanity in planned or accidental self-destruction.

We dare not tempt them with weakness. For only when our arms are sufficient beyond doubt can we be certain beyond doubt that they will never be employed.

But neither can two great and powerful groups of nations take comfort from our present course—both sides overburdened by the cost of modern weapons, both rightly alarmed by the steady spread of the deadly atom, yet both racing to alter that uncertain balance of terror that stays the hand of mankind's final war.

So let us begin anew—remembering on both sides that civility is not a sign of weakness, and sincerity is always subject to proof. Let us never negotiate out of fear. But let us never fear to negotiate.

Let both sides explore what problems unite us instead of belaboring those problems which divide us. Let both sides, for the first time, formulate serious and precise proposals for the inspection and control of arms—and bring the absolute power to destroy other nations under the absolute control of all nations.

Let both sides seek to invoke the wonders of science instead of its terrors. Together let us explore the stars, conquer the deserts, eradicate disease, tap the ocean depths and encourage the arts and commerce.

Let both sides unite to heed in all corners of the earth the command of Isaiah—to "undo the heavy burdens. . .(and) let the oppressed go free."

And if a beach-head of cooperation may push back the jungle of suspicion, let both sides join in a new endeavor, not a new balance of power, but a new world of law, where the strong are just and the weak secure and the peace preserved.

All this will not be finished in the first one hundred days. Nor will it be finished in the first one thousand days, nor in the life of this Administration, nor even perhaps in our lifetime on this planet. But let us begin.

In your hands, my fellow citizens, more than mine, will rest the final success or failure of our course. Since this country was founded, each generation of Americans has been summoned to give testimony to its national loyalty. The graves of young Americans who answered the call to service surround the globe.

Now the trumpet summons us again—not as a call to bear arms, though arms we need—not as a call to battle, though embattled we are—but a call to bear the burden of a long twilight struggle, year in and year out, "rejoicing in hope, patient in tribulation"—a struggle against the common enemies of man: tyranny, poverty, disease and war itself.

Can we forge against these enemies a grand and global alliance, North and South, East and West, that can assure a more fruitful life for all mankind? Will you join in that historic effort?

In the long history of the world, only a few generations have been granted the role of defending freedom in its hour of maximum danger. I do not shrink from this responsibility—I welcome it. I do not believe that any of us would exchange places with any other people or any other generation. The energy, the faith, the devotion which we bring to this endeavor will light our country and all who serve it—and the glow from that fire can truly light the world.

And so, my fellow Americans: Ask not what your country can do for you—ask what you can do for your country.

My fellow citizens of the world: Ask not what America will do for you, but what together we can do for the freedom of man.

Finally, whether you are citizens of America or citizens of the world, ask of us here the same high standards of strength and sacrifice which we ask of you. With a good conscience our only sure reward, with history the final judge of our deeds, let us go forth to lead the land we love, asking His blessing and His help, but knowing that here on earth God's work must truly be our own.

# Questioning the Motives and Goals of the Peace Corps

## By Alice-Leone Moats

On March 1, 1961, President Kennedy signed an executive order establishing the Peace Corps as a "pool of trained American men and women sent overseas by the U.S. Government . . . to help foreign countries meet their urgent needs for skilled manpower." The new organization was to recruit and train volunteers with specialized skills and place them in positions of leadership in developing nations. Once abroad, the recruits would teach in the schools, implement sanitation and engineering projects, and generally work to improve local living conditions. The president's announcement captured the imagination of many young people, who viewed the Corps as an opportunity to serve the cause of social progress in needy countries while satisfying a yearning for travel and adventure.

Kennedy's adversaries, however, greeted the Peace Corps with skepticism and questioned whether it was not simply a disingenuous weapon with which to fight the Cold War. In the following April 1961 editorial, which appeared in the conservative *National Review* magazine, Alice-Leone Moats contends that the Corps deserves greater public scrutiny. According to Moats, many important details remain ill considered, and most important, foreign nations have not expressed much enthusiasm for the presence of volunteers. The author, who died

Alice-Leone Moats, "Peace, It's Wonderful," *National Review*, vol. 10, April 8, 1961, pp. 211–12. Copyright © 1961 by National Review, Inc., 215 Lexington Ave., New York, NY 10016. Reproduced by permission.

in 1989, wrote frequently for the *Philadelphia Inquirer* and served as a
foreign correspondent for *Collier's* magazine.

I f the Peace Corps had been a new slimming compound it
couldn't have been launched with more superlatives more
promises of quick and lasting results, more assurances that
it would kill all ills. And, as usual, the public has fallen for the
fancy doubletalk and is ready to buy the advertised product without
asking questions.

## Preparing the Pilot Project

In this case, it is perhaps just as well because nobody connected
with the Peace Corps appears to have done enough homework to
know the answers. President Kennedy's brother-in-law, R. Sargent
Shriver, who won quick confirmation from the Senate Foreign Relations
Committee as director of the newly-created government
agency, held a press conference on March 6 [1961], which shed
little light on the future activities of the Peace Corps. His answers
to questions either began or ended with such phrases as, "I'd just
like to make one comment, and it is that all of the things here are
in the tentative planning stage," or, "Yes, we plan to do that, but
like everything else in the Peace Corps, it's flexible."

In spite of tentative planning and flexibility, however, preparations
are already under way for a pilot project that will put 500
to a thousand volunteers in training at the beginning of June and
have them overseas by the end of the year. Twenty thousand
questionnaires have been sent out to people who wrote indicating
a desire to serve as unpaid workers abroad. They are four
pages long and require information as to the skills and abilities
of the applicant. Nothing has been overlooked—from a talent for
languages to a talent for operating a bulldozer; from expertness
in folk dancing to expertise in handling equipment for canning;
from knowledge about the world in general and certain countries
in particular, to an aptitude for football.

The applicants who get over this first hurdle will be interviewed
by panels made up of "interested citizens" and there may
even be a written test; that has not yet been decided. Finally, the
best candidates will be chosen by the officials at headquarters in
Washington. It is estimated that only one out of ten aspirants can
make the grade.

## Core for the Corps

The training is to be given at "six or a dozen" American colleges and universities and will last four or six months. What Mr. Shriver terms the "core curriculum" will be made up of courses in American institutions, philosophy and democratic government; economics; the culture and customs of the country to which a volunteer is to be assigned; languages. Mr. Shriver has been assured by "linguistic experts that even exotic languages can be learned to a reasonably good point in four or five months if you concentrate hard enough, and that is what we will try to do."

Besides the "core curriculum" there are to be courses for those preparing to specialize in teaching, or engineering, or plumbing, or whatever.

Mr. Shriver allayed any fears that the shortage of teachers in this country might be aggravated by drawing them into the Peace Corps when he explained that a "large number of trained educators have confirmed our belief that a graduate of an accredited American institution of higher education would have no difficulty in teaching English as a second language, in learning to teach English as a second language, in a high-pressure, if you will, training program of four months duration." It is obvious that the trained educators who reach that conclusion did not first try to parse one of Mr. Shriver's English sentences!

A volunteer must be over eighteen and agree to serve for at least one year besides the training period. It is hoped that most of the boys and girls will remain two years, but anybody is free to quit if he isn't happy. The tentative maximum term is three years. Although no salaries are to be paid, all expenses for food, housing, clothing and travel will be covered "to provide volunteers with a standard of living commensurate with the country in which they are living and the work that they are doing." In plain English this means that a school teacher, for instance, who lands in Nigeria will receive enough money to live in the same style as a Nigerian school teacher, or a road builder who is sent to Burma will enjoy the same comforts as a coolie. So far, nobody seems to have ventured to point out that in Asia and Africa, a foreigner who goes native loses face, and once he has lost face, he can't teach anybody anything.

A bonus of fifty or seventy-five dollars a month—the exact figure hasn't been decided—is to be paid to each volunteer, but not in the field; these sums will accumulate to form a nest egg that will tide over the homecoming pioneer while he finds a job. A group of eminent men representing labor, industry, government and education is prepared to contribute its time and energy towards developing appropriate job opportunities for all volunteers returning to "civilian status." And, as Mr. Shriver puts it, "The Public Health Service has graciously agreed to accept the responsibility for the care of the Peace Corps volunteers in this country and while they are abroad." That, clearly, is expected to dispose of any risk of Buster coming home with several unpronounceable diseases and a couple that aren't pronounced in polite society.

## It's Flexible

So, the broad outlines have been sketched in, but precisely what these New Look pioneers are to do once their covered wagons start rolling across deserts and through jungles hasn't yet been decided. It's flexible. No definite project can be worked out until it is known exactly where they will be sent. The general idea is that they are to teach English, to help build roads, set up sewage and irrigation systems, instruct the natives of underdeveloped countries in modern techniques and also teach them how to live. When the latter aim was announced, a Mr. Edmond A. Gibson wrote a letter to the *Washington Star* asking, "Is it possible that this notion can be seriously entertained?" After giving an unflattering picture of the average American college graduate, he ended, "I don't know about the citizens of other lands, but if anyone suggested to me that I allow one of these half-wits to teach me how to live I would consider the suggestion a personal insult."

Although so far no foreign nation has declared that it has been insulted, neither have there been any indications of wild enthusiasm for the presence of Peace Corps volunteers. Mr. Shriver, when asked how many countries had expressed a desire—officially or unofficially—to have some pioneers sent to them, answered that there had been about ten or a dozen, but he wouldn't specify which ones.

Nobody at the press conference inquired what precaution would be taken to prevent the infiltration of Communists into the Peace Corps. At headquarters, I was told that I might be right in believing that the Communists would be greatly tempted to take such an organization over, but I mustn't worry—all applicants would be thoroughly investigated. I pointed out that a thorough investigation takes several months and it was explained that each applicant will be screened during the training period; if any candidate isn't given a clearance, he will be dropped without explanation. The Peace Corps is in a hurry to get the show on the road and the hell with bothering about details like a waste of time or expense.

The possibility of sex rearing its busy little head has also been taken into consideration. The unofficial attitude on this question is to accept the facts of life unless they become too obvious. In other words, any Peace Corps missionary unwise enough to engage in public sin with one of the natives he or she has gone to redeem, will promptly be shipped home.

## A Lack of Skilled Volunteers

The problem the optimists at headquarters don't seem to be prepared to face is the difficulty of finding college graduates with the technical training that would be useful to the Peace Corps, who will be willing to abandon their careers at the outset or in mid-stream in order to go hooting off to distant lands as unpaid workers. And, even if some are rash enough to do it, will they be allowed to use their skills in countries where labor laws forbid the hiring of foreigners? The answer to that is "We hope to be able to come to some agreement with the local unions."

Nothing is to be allowed to stand in the way of this pioneer corps which would certainly puzzle the original pioneers if they could return to earth and see it. They would not understand the new frontiersmen who are setting forth in groups under the watchful eye of a supervisor, all arrangements made and all expenses paid by a benevolent government; their health cared for by a gracious Public Health Service and their return to comfortable homes guaranteed.

In a little speech that opened the press conference, Mr. Shriver said, "I hope that the Peace Corps is going to take a lot of people by surprise." Everything certainly indicates that this wish of his will be fulfilled: a lot of people are going to be surprised and nobody more than the citizens of underdeveloped countries who are about to be taught to live by a Peace Corps.

# The Failed Invasion of Cuba at the Bay of Pigs

### By the *Nation*

On April 17, 1961, President Kennedy ordered a brigade of 1,500 armed Cuban exiles to land in Cuba's Bay of Pigs with the goal of instigating a popular uprising against Communist dictator Fidel Castro. The vastly outnumbered brigade, which had been trained and recruited by the U.S. Central Intelligence Agency (CIA), was immediately overwhelmed by Castro's forces—103 were killed and 1,189 were taken prisoner. The invasion led to the arrest of 2,500 CIA agents and 20,000 anti-Castro rebels inside Cuba, galvanizing Castro's efforts to eliminate what remained of his political opposition.

The president's reasons for ordering the invasion arose from the unfavorable political situation in Cuba, an island nation located just forty miles from the Florida coast. In January 1959, Castro had waged a successful coup against unpopular dictator Fulgencio Batista and, within a year, had declared himself a Communist. This announcement brought Cuba's status as an important U.S. trading partner to an abrupt end, and by 1960, then-president Dwight D. Eisenhower had imposed tough economic sanctions. Needing a new economic sponsor, Castro forged a diplomatic alliance with the Soviet Union, a development viewed as a serious threat to U.S. security and a huge shift in the Western Hemisphere's balance of power.

"What System, Please?" *The Nation*, vol. 192, May 6, 1961, pp. 381–83. Copyright © 1961 by The Nation Company, Inc. Reproduced by permission.

Kennedy was roundly criticized for ordering the invasion, which is regarded by many historians as a critical foreign policy blunder. In the following editorial that appeared in the *Nation*, a liberal political journal, the authors contend that the president has undermined the democratic process by conducting a covert war without congressional approval. The result, in the author's opinion, is that Cold War tensions have been aggravated, and U.S. interests in the region have been imperiled.

**"L**et me then make clear," said Mr. Kennedy to the American Society of Newspaper Editors [on April 20, 1961, in Washington, D.C.], "as the President of the United States that I am determined upon our system's survival and success, regardless of the cost and regardless of the peril." When he utters such portentous words, it is well for a head of state to know precisely what he purposes to defend and to be sure that he does not lose it in the process of defending it. Mr. Kennedy has already gone some distance in that direction. What is the system on whose behalf he is prepared to stake all? It is, first, a government of laws, not of men. Yet, in organizing the invasion of Cuba, the Central Intelligence Agency [CIA] has broken international conventions and domestic statutes without hindrance and without compunction. Then, we are a democracy, in which the elected representatives of the people supposedly disburse public funds, oversee the operations of government bodies and, in extremity, declare war. The Central Intelligence Agency has usurped the functions of the Congress in waging a preventive war with Mr. Kennedy's approval, and so far, with the exception of Senators Wayne Morse and Eugene McCarthy, the Congress has sat mute. We are said to be an open society, in which the press reports the news and is free to praise, criticize or condemn. In this open society, by this mechanism, the government is to be responsible to public opinion. Actually, public opinion has ceased to function, for the government proceeded in secrecy, most of the press abetted it, and the public was faced with a *fait accompli* and invited to rally around the flag.

## The CIA: An Undemocratic Institution

All this bears but scant resemblance to the American system as understood by the Founding Fathers and their descendants, all the way down to Mr. Kennedy himself. What it does resemble closely is the theory and practice of communism, save in one respect—it isn't as effective. Except for this rather crucial difference, the proverbial visitor from Mars could scarcely distinguish between the performance of the CIA in the Cuban fiasco and the tactics of infiltration, subversion and insurrection laid at the door of "international communism." He would behold the CIA, a body responsible only to the executive arm of the government, carrying on intelligence operations all over the world, many of them involving espionage, sabotage and violence. In the past few years it has overthrown governments (Guatemala, Iran), shored up dictatorships (South Vietnam, Thailand, etc.) and now it has gone so far as to make war by proxy under its almost unlimited powers. It doles out some bits of information, at its own discretion, to selected members of Congress, but in a government of checks and balances it goes unchecked and unquestioned.

And all this, judging by the examples that have come to light, is done badly. This agency, so trusted by the President that he reappointed its director as his first act after being elected to the office, made so many mistakes in the Cuban operation that one can only conclude that its highest officials are addicted to pathologically wishful thinking. But perhaps there is an underlying reason for their blunders which is less to their discredit. Perhaps the entire concept is so alien to the system which the President is sworn to defend that malfunctions are the expression of an irrepressible conflict between democracy and an egregiously undemocratic institution. How can we expect to plot surreptitious warfare in a country in which not all the press can be stifled, in which dissidents cannot be thrown in jail *en masse*, in which absolute unanimity of opinion cannot be enforced, and in which fear can be induced in only a minor part of the population? Mr. Kennedy may be thankful that the conditions have proved so unpropitious for the adventure on which he was persuaded to embark; it is an indication that the American ethos remains more than a tissue of catchwords. Ours is a way of life which, God knows, has at times been practiced imperfectly enough; let the President enumerate for himself those times and avoid those errors. Let him ponder on the essentials of the system he says he holds dear. Arms and armaments will not avail him, but only the application of the principles which guided the Republic in the times of Washington, of Jefferson, of Lincoln and, not least, and not long ago, of Franklin D. Roosevelt.

## The Disaster Button

Long-continued national frustration is dangerous, and the more powerful the nation, the greater the danger. The United States has had its share of distasteful and humiliating experiences since the close of World War II—the Stalin advance in Europe, the Soviet acquisition of the hydrogen bomb before we developed ours, the first Sputnik, the first Soviet planetary shots, the U-2 incident, the first Russian man in space, Laos, and now the Cuban fiasco. Nerves are rasped and tempers are getting short, and at this juncture we have a President who, as the conservative *Figaro* of Paris pointed out, is stronger in dynamism than in wisdom or experience. It is all-important, then, to acknowledge that our misfortunes have been our own doing, and are not the unmerited blows of fate. In the Cuban debacle, particularly, we asked for exactly what we got. Equally important, all of us—and the President in particular—must control the impulse to act through force. Belligerence, as such, will only enmesh us more deeply in a situation that is already bad enough.

There are signs that the President does not appreciate this, and further, that he has been less than candid. On April 13 [1961] he promised that there would be no direct American intervention in

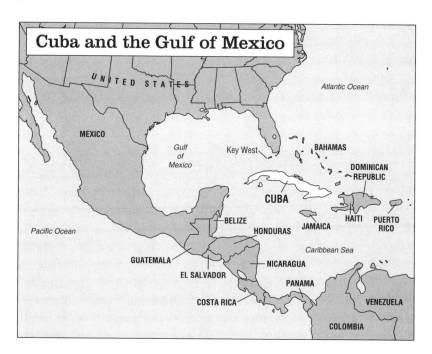

Cuba and the Gulf of Mexico

Cuba under any circumstances. We now know that this statement had an operational purpose—it was a cover for the commando raid by Cuban counterrevolutionaries under the maladroit direction of the CIA. The disaster which engulfed the invasion and, ironically, the fantastic overpublicizing of its magnitude, now increases the likelihood of a far rasher venture. Stung by the defeat of "our" Cubans (whom the CIA had carefully screened to eliminate left-wing elements), our pride injured, our humiliation compounded by the incredible mismanagement displayed for all the world to see, we now stand in danger of doing what the President assured us we would not do "under any circumstances," i.e., regress to the level of the Marine or Dollar Diplomacy of the Harding-Coolidge era. Verbally, the regression has already occurred. In one of the most belligerent and reckless speeches ever made by an American President [an April 20, 1961, address to the American Society of Newspaper Editors in Washington, D.C.], Mr. Kennedy openly threatened our uneasy Latin American allies:

> . . . if the nations of this Hemisphere should fail to meet their commitments against outside Communist penetration, then I want it clearly understood that this Government will not hesitate in meeting its primary obligations, which are the security of our nation.

In short, and unmistakably, we will go it alone. The only glimmer of prudence in this arm-twisting oration was that it did not set a time limit.

## A Dissenting Voice

Mr. Kennedy might avail himself of Senator Wayne Morse's speech on "The Situation in Cuba" (*Congressional Record*, April 24, pp. 6,179–6,187) for purposes of tranquilization and political guidance. Speaking as chairman of the Senate Subcommittee on Latin American Affairs, Mr. Morse quoted a telegram he had sent to the Secretary of State, protesting the Administration's failure to advise with the subcommittee before plunging into the Cuban embroilment. Expressing his own "hatred and detestation of what Castro stands for," Senator Morse pointed out that this did not alter the fact that Castro heads the sovereign government of Cuba, and that it is entitled to all the rights under existing law of signatories to the Charter of the Organization of American States. He rejected the argument that we must meet fire with fire, that we must beat the Communists at their own game. He ridiculed the argument that Cuba constitutes a military threat to the United States; this is of a piece with Hitler's assertion that Czechoslovakia was a dagger pointed at the heart of Germany. And then Mr. Morse issued this warning:

> I say to Senators today that it is my judgment that if the United States seeks to settle its differences with Cuba through the use of military might, either direct or indirect, we shall be at least a half century recovering, if we ever recover, the prestige, the understanding, the sympathy, and the confidence of one Latin American neighbor after another.

The American press buried the speech; few papers gave it any notice whatsoever. Mr. Kennedy would be well advised to read it.

## History Will Not Absolve Him

President Kennedy might well consider why President Eisenhower was so popular that, in his wake, he nearly ensconced Richard M. Nixon as his successor. Popularity is not the final test of a President but, in a democracy, it contributes to his success and cannot be thrown out with a pitchfork. If Mr. Kennedy finds himself as popular after his four years (or eight), he may account himself fortunate indeed. How, then, did General Eisenhower gain such a secure place in the hearts of his countrymen? Psychoanalytic "images" aside, it was largely because he was unmistakably a man of peace.

Mr. Kennedy has given some signs of wishing to follow General Eisenhower's footsteps along this path; in fact, in some respects he has improved on his predecessor. He shut up the blowhard generals and admirals and elevated diplomatic intercourse to a higher plane, without the pointless abuse of some of the Eisenhower ambassadors. In a spirit of tentative reconnoitering, he began an exploration of the possibilities of a *modus vivendi* with the Soviets. Although all this could be regarded as consistent with a resolution to prosecute the cold war as before, only more efficiently and resolutely, it was also consistent with a creative peace effort and, as such, welcome.

This hope was disrupted by the Cuban adventure and its aftermath. Now, many thoughtful Americans will deduce that if Kennedy had had any real heart for an alleviation of cold-war tensions, he would have held off on his preventive war until his exploratory efforts had had a fair chance. The two courses were clearly inconsistent. Instead, he gave the CIA, and Messrs. Adolf A. Berle, Jr., and Arthur Schlesinger, Jr., a free hand to topple Castro. The result we know. It was first reported, later denied (but it is almost certainly true), that Messrs. [Dean] Rusk [secretary of state] and [Chester] Bowles [special adviser on Latin America] were in opposition. Now, as loyal members of the team, they are as compromised as their colleagues. It is a bad setback for an Administration that began with better manners and more erudition than the preceding one.

If this does not chasten Mr. Kennedy, another factor merits his consideration. He is a progressive politician, more in the tradition of, say, [former Democratic president] Franklin D. Roosevelt, than, say, [former Republican president] Herbert Hoover. The last thing he wants is to unleash the forces of the frenetic Right, always latent in the American setup and now inflamed by American reverses. He has spoken out against the John Birch Society [a group of right-wing conservatives] and set in motion proceedings against General Edwin A. Walker who, if not a member of the organization, apparently propagandized along similar lines. If any of the reports of impending American action against Castro prove accurate—if we attack him directly, or prepare another assault by proxy, or try to strangle him economically by blockade or further economic sanctions—it will be a godsend to the lunatic fringe exemplified by the John Birch fanatics. The President may not welcome them as allies, but he will be in bed with them just the same.

What, then, would we have the President do? *The Nation* does not hesitate to offer Mr. Kennedy advice, since its articles have accurately predicted the course of events in Cuba since Castro set foot in the Sierra Maestra. *The Nation* urges Mr. Kennedy to stay out of Cuba, to cease intervention of any kind whatsoever. Let the "commando" groups be disbanded. Instruct the Attorney General [Robert F. Kennedy] to enforce the neutrality laws. Padlock the cloak-and-dagger "spooks" at the CIA. Avoid a blockade. Heed carefully the well-considered advice of Senators Morse, Fulbright and McCarthy. Let the dust settle. Any further violence on the part of the American government, whether by subornation or directly, will be a disaster for the United States and, before history, for Mr. Kennedy himself.

# The First American Astronaut in Space

### By Alan B. Shepard

Navy commander Alan B. Shepard became the first American to travel into space on the morning of May 5, 1961, landing safely in the Atlantic Ocean after a fifteen-minute suborbital flight. At the time of his voyage, the United States was trailing the Soviet Union in the "space race"—the battle between the superpowers to prove their superior science and technology through space exploration. Not only had the Soviets launched the first satellite, *Sputnik I*, in 1957, Soviet astronaut Yuri Gagarin had successfully completed the first-ever manned space flight on April 12, 1961, beating the Americans by four weeks. Winning the space race was of prime concern to President Kennedy, and Shepard's flight was viewed as a much-needed boost to the U.S. space program. In his May 25, 1961, State of the Union address, Kennedy requested additional funding to expand the space program and announced that the nation would land a man on the moon before the close of the decade.

In the following first-person narrative, Alan B. Shepard recalls the moments leading up to the launch of the Project Mercury space capsule, *Freedom 7*, the exhilarating sensations of liftoff, the view from space, and the long plunge back to Earth. In 1971, Shepard commanded *Apollo 14* on its flight to the moon and was the fifth man to set foot on the lunar surface.

At a little after 1 o'clock Friday morning, [May 5, 1961,] I got up, shaved and showered and had steak and eggs for breakfast with John [Glenn, Project Mercury's backup

Alan B. Shepard, "The Astronaut's Story of the Thrust into Space," *Life*, vol. 50, May 12, 1961, pp. 26–28, 30–31. Copyright © 1961 by Time, Inc. Reproduced by permission.

astronaut] and our flight surgeon, Dr. Bill Douglas. Gus Grissom came in and so did Walt Williams and Shorty Powers, the Mercury public affairs officer. Everything still looked fine. We joked around a bit. After the final medical exam the doctors taped on the sensors that would tell them my physiological reactions before and during the flight and I suited up. There were butterflies in my stomach now but I didn't feel at all that I was coming apart or that things were getting ahead of me. The adrenalin was surely pumping but my blood pressure and pulse rate were not unusually high.

At 4 we left the hangar, got into the transfer van and drove out to the gantry. Inside the van I relaxed in a reclining chair. Finally everything was ready and I walked out to the gleaming Redstone and rode up in the elevator. On the way up Bill Douglas suddenly handed me a box of crayons. This was a real tension breaker. In the last weeks we'd all heard a comic record about an Astronaut who wouldn't go into space without taking along the crayons and coloring book to pass away the time. I thought I'd be too busy to use the crayons on this flight, but I had a good laugh as I handed them back.

## I Wanted to Thank John

Topside, in the green plastic penthouse that covered the capsule, preparations were almost completed. I walked around a bit, chatted briefly with Gus Grissom and John Glenn. I wanted especially to thank John for all the hard work he'd done as my backup. He'd just completed his final check in the cockpit. Some of the crew looked a little tense up there but none of the Astronauts showed it.

It was 5:20, time to get into the capsule. There, inside where no one but the pilot could see it, I found a final, pre-launch joke. Attached to the instrument panel was a little notice that read: NO HANDBALL PLAYING IN THIS AREA. When he saw me laugh behind the visor, John Glenn grinned, reached in and pulled down the sign.

The countdown proceeded. My straps were all checked, the final connections were made into my suit. Different heads and hands kept popping through the opening to make last-minute adjustments. Then at 6:10 the hatch was closed and I was alone. . . .

I went through all the checkoff lists, tested the radio systems and the gyro switches. The tension slacked off immediately. As I worked, I could look out through the periscope viewer in the center of the instrument panel and see the crew working around the outside of the capsule. Nearly all of them stopped as they passed the other end of the periscope and peeked in at me. Round and distorted, their faces were close and friendly as they loomed up on my screen.

When the gantry rolled back at 6:34, the view through the periscope was fascinating. I could see clouds in the sky and people working far below me on the ground. The rising sun came up right into the scope, getting so bright that I had to crank in some filters to cut down the glare.

## A Little Electrical Trouble

With the count at T-15, we had a delay because of clouds in the Cape [Canaveral, Florida,] area. Then, while we were still holding for weather, there was trouble with a small electrical component in the booster and the gantry was rolled back around me so the crew could replace it. During this delay, which lasted a total of 86 minutes, I continued to feel fine. The doctors could tell how I was doing by instruments and there was never any doubt. . . .

We had another hold at T-2 minutes 40 seconds and here I got a little impatient. I'd been in the capsule more than three hours now, and I was ready to go. Hearing the deliberate, careful voices discussing this new problem, which involved one of the computers, I was strongly tempted to get into the act myself and urge everybody along. But I decided that their caution might benefit me in the long run and I kept quiet. The count picked up again.

At T-2 I got my final transmission from the blockhouse, set the control valves for the suit and the cabin temperatures and began talking to Deke Slayton in the control center. . . .

At T-35 seconds I watched through the periscope as the umbilical connection, which had fed power and air into the capsule, was pulled out and fell away. Now the capsule was on its own power. The top of the periscope retracted, the covering door closed and the good view I'd had all morning was temporarily gone. I wouldn't be able to see anything again until I was in space. I reported "periscope in" and the fact that the voltage and current readings for the batteries which now ran the capsule systems were both in GO condition. I heard Deke say "Roger" and then listened to his count run down from 10 seconds. My right hand was up to start a stopwatch exactly at liftoff, and my left hand was on the abort handle, which I was ready to throw if there was trouble on the launch.

The count reached zero.

I must admit that I braced myself too much for that marvelous liftoff. There was nobody around to tell me how it would actually feel and we hadn't heard about it from Moscow. I had tensed myself against the vibration and shock and I'd even turned up the volume on my headphones near full power so that I could hear transmissions through the noise. When the bird lighted I could hear a rumble beneath me and feel the vibration but both were at a much lower level than I expected. As I called out, "Liftoff and the clock has started," I was really exhilarated and surprised. It was smooth, gradual and gentle. There was no question about the fact that I was going. That was certain. I could see it on the instruments, hear it on the headphones, feel it all around me. My trip had finally started but it had started in an astonishingly pleasant way.

## An Air of Familiarity

For the first minute the ride continued smooth and my main job was to keep the people on the ground as relaxed and informed as I could. I reported that everything was functioning perfectly, that all the systems were working, that the Gs [gravitational forces] were mounting slightly as predicted. The long hours of rehearsal had helped. It was almost as if I had been there before. It was enormously strange and exciting, but my earlier practice gave the whole thing a comfortable air of familiarity. Deke's clear transmissions in my headphones reassured me still more.

One minute after liftoff the bird rode a little rough. At this point in the flight the booster and capsule passed from subsonic to supersonic speed and then immediately went through the zone of maximum dynamic pressure where the forces of air density and speed combine at their peak. There was a good bit of vibration and buffeting.

We had known that this was going to happen but it was a little heavier than I thought it would be. I never considered getting out. I tried to focus on the cabin pressure reading. I thought briefly about reporting the buffeting but then decided against it. A garbled transmission about vibration at that point might have sent everybody on the ground into a state of shock. I didn't want to leave or have anyone make any quick decision that I should leave. My mind had probably been made up unconsciously in advance to handle things alone if I could and call for help only if I couldn't. The vibration stopped and we were through in one piece. I called to Deke. "O.K. It is a lot smoother now. A lot smoother."

The cabin pressure was holding at 5.5 pounds per square inch just as it had been designed to do. At two minutes after launch, at an altitude of about 25 miles, the Gs were building as I climbed at a speed of about 2,700 mph. The ride was now fine, just exactly as we had planned. I made my last radio transmission before the booster engine cut off: "All systems are GO."

The cutoff occurred right on schedule. Nothing abrupt happened. As the fuel burned out in the chamber there was a gradual drop in the level of forward thrust, all very smooth. Then I heard a roaring noise when the escape tower, now no longer needed, was blown off. I'd hoped before the flight that I'd notice smoke going past the portholes when this happened but I was too busy keeping track of events on the instrument panel to look. Separation of the capsule from the booster, a point I'd thought about quite a lot in the past, was coming up now. I heard the noise of the separation rockets as they fired and saw the verifying light flash green on the panel. I don't recall thinking anything in particular at separation, but there's good medical evidence that I was concerned about it at the time. My pulse rate reached its peak here, 132, and started down afterward.

Right after separation the capsule and I went weightless. I could feel the capsule begin its slow, lazy turnaround as the autopilot pivoted it 180° so that the blunt end faced forward. The periscope came out but, though I was aware of land and clouds and movement in the viewer, I didn't really look. I still had a most important function before I could stop to enjoy the view. We wanted to see if the pilot could control the capsule in space and this was the time to begin.

Up to that point the free and weightless capsule, traveling at 4,500 miles an hour, had been flown by the autopilot. Now using my three-axis control stick, I switched over to manual control, one axis at a time. First I tried controlling the pitch axis and found I could easily raise or lower the blunt end of the capsule. The instruments recorded the movements. Each time I moved the stick little jets of hydrogen peroxide popped off on the outside of the capsule and pushed it the way I wanted to go. Then I fed in the yaw axis to my hand controller and it worked too. Finally I took over control of the roll motion of the capsule and was flying Freedom 7 on my own. This was a big moment for me and for everybody who had worked so hard on Project Mercury. Major Gagarin may have had a fine long ride but, as far as we can tell, he was a passenger all the way.

Now was the time to go to the periscope. I'd been well briefed; I knew what to expect in the way of land masses, cloud cover and color. But no one could be briefed well enough not to be astonished at the view I got from 100 miles up. My exclamation back to Deke about the beautiful sight was completely spontaneous. It was breathtaking.

To the south I could see that the cloud cover stopped around Fort Lauderdale and that the weather was clear all the way down past the Florida Keys. To the north I could see up the coast of the Carolinas to where Cape Hatteras was obscured by clouds. Across Florida to the west I saw Tampa Bay and Pensacola and easily spotted Lake Okeechobee. Because there were now scattered clouds far beneath me, I was not able to see some of the Bahama Islands I had been briefed to look for, so I shifted my view to an open area and found that I could identify Andros Island and Bimini. The colors around the ocean islands below were brilliantly clear and the variations were sharp between the blue of deep water and the light green of the shoal areas around the reefs.

For a while then, using Cape Canaveral as a heading, I flew the capsule by looking through the periscope instead of at the instruments and found that this was not at all difficult. Even if the instruments and autopilot should fail on a later flight, we now know we can handle the capsule another way. . . .

Near the apogee of my flight, at about 115 miles of altitude, I began to hear Deke's countdown for the firing of the retro-rockets. In an orbital flight these braking rockets would be necessary to begin the return to earth but here we were just testing them and my reactions to their firing. No matter what happened now on this flight I'd drop back down on a regular ballistic trajectory.

## A Small, Upsetting Motion

Still using the hand controller, I tilted the blunt end of the capsule up to an angle of 34° above the horizon, and at five minutes and 11 seconds after launch the first of the three retro-rockets fired. There was just a small, upsetting motion as our speed was slowed and I was pushed back into the couch a bit. But, as the rockets fired in sequence, each time pushing the capsule somewhat off its proper angle, I brought it back. Perhaps the most encouraging product of the trip was the way I was able to stay on top of the flight by using manual controls.

We were on the way down now and I got set for the jettisoning of the used retros which were attached to the blunt end of the capsule. The retro package blew off right on time. I could feel it go and through the periscope I could see part of the strapping fall away. But the jettison light did not change to green on the panel. This was our only circuit failure in the whole flight and when I pushed an override button that acts as a backup, the light turned green as it was supposed to do.

Now I brought the capsule into its re-entry attitude, front end pointing downward at an angle of 40°, and switched over to the autopilot. The flight was more than half over and I hadn't yet had a chance to look out the porthole for the planets I hoped to spot. But it was now too late in the morning for me to see them. I could not find them through the eight-inch porthole and I didn't have time to maneuver the capsule around for a more thorough look. Still, the view through the right-hand port was spectacular. The sky was very dark blue and the clouds a brilliant white. Between me and the clouds was something that looked like haze; it was the refraction of the sun's light on the various layers of the atmosphere.

The re-entry G forces built up and hit me a little before I was quite ready for them. Because I wanted to try some hand controlling before we got too deeply back into the atmosphere, I was pretty busy for a moment running around the cockpit changing from the automatic pilot to the manual system. I got in a few corrective movements before the heavy air forces overcame the effect of the control jets.

## Clear All the Way

In that long plunge back to earth I was pushed back into the couch with a force about 10 times the pull of gravity. We've all experienced much higher Gs on the centrifuge at Johnsville, Pennsylvania, and I remember being clear all the way through the re-entry. I was able to report the G level with normal voice procedure and I never reached the point, as I often had in the centrifuge, where I had to use the maximum amount of effort to speak or even to breathe.

All the way down, as the altimeter spun through mile after mile of descent, I granted out O.K., O.K., O.K. just to show them how I was doing. Throughout this period of descent the capsule rolled very slowly in a counterclockwise direction, spinning at 10° a second. This had no noticeable reflect on me, and neither did the heat which, though it built up to 1,500° on the outside wall, only climbed to 102° in the cabin and 78° in the suit. But then we never thought that heat would be a problem until we got to orbital flight. The life support system—oxygen, water coolers, ventilators, the suit itself—all worked without a hitch. At worst it was like being in a closed car on a warm summer day. As the G forces dropped and we reached about 80,000 feet, I switched back to the autopilot.

By the time I reached 30,000 feet the capsule had slowed to about 300 mph. I had known all along from talking to Deke that my trajectory was good and that Freedom 7 was going to hit right in the center of the recovery area. But a lot of things still had to happen before I could stretch out and take it easy. I began to concentrate quite heavily on the parachutes.

A small stabilizing chute called a drogue is supposed to come out of the neck of the capsule at 21,000 feet. Right about this time the periscope, which had been retracted during re-entry, came out again too. Sure enough, the first thing I saw against the sky in my viewer was this little drogue, streaming out white about the size of a silver dollar in the top of the scope. So far, so good. At 15,000 feet a ventilation valve opened on schedule and cool fresh air came into the capsule. The main chute was yet to come.

This invaluable aid to the weary space traveler is supposed to make its appearance at 10,000 feet. If it fails to show, the pilot can break out the reserve chute by pulling a ring on the instrument panel. I must admit my finger was right on the ring as we passed through 10,000 feet. But I didn't need to pull. Through the periscope I could watch a whole beautiful sequence start taking place.

I saw a small canister released from the top of the capsule and get pulled away by the drogue chute. Then the canister in its turn pulled out the bag that held the main chute. The bag slipped off and all of a sudden there it was, the main chute stretched out long and thin and not yet opened against the sky. Four seconds later the brilliant orange and white canopy bloomed above me. It looked wonderful. I stared at it through the periscope for signs of trouble. It was drawing perfectly. A glance at my rate-of-descent indicator on the instrument panel proved that I had a good chute. This was a moment of high relief for me. In fact I felt great.

The water landing was still ahead and I started getting ready for it. I opened the face plate in the helmet and disconnected the hose that keeps the visor sealed when the suit is pressurized. I took off my knee straps and released the strap that went across my chest. During the descent the capsule swung gently back and forth under the chute. At about 1,000 feet, I looked out the port and saw we were getting close to the water. I didn't see the pickup helicopters but assumed they were nearby. I braced myself for the impact.

The landing was abrupt but no more upsetting than we'd expected. The capsule dug into the water and went over on its right side to an angle of about 60° or 70°. I was pushed down into the couch and then over to the right. The right porthole went underwater immediately and stayed there. I hit the switch that was supposed to kick out the reserve chute. This would take some of the weight off the top of the capsule and eventually help it right itself. The same switch would start the sequence to deploy a high frequency radio antenna. Other recovery aids—dye markers, a sonar depth bomb—were working. I sat back and watched things happen.

## All Kinds of Gurgling

I knew that in about a minute the capsule should swing back into an upright position. If not, there could be a little difficulty. There seemed to be no water coming in anywhere, but there were all kinds of gurgling sounds and there might, for all I knew then, have been small leaks. But there was clearly nothing big.

At this point I remember feeling, "Well, O.K., you're in good shape now. If you have to get out that side door there, underwater, you've done it before in practice and you know you can do it now." But I was pleased to see that the capsule was slowly swinging to its proper position. As soon as I knew the radio antenna was well clear of the water, I sent a message that I was on the water and all right.

I took off my lap belt and loosened my helmet so that I could take it off when I went out the door. Leaving the capsule for the helicopter had been the plan all the way. I was getting ready to take a final reading on all the capsule instruments when the chopper pilot called and said that he was right above me, getting ready to hook on. I skipped the instrument reading because it seemed more important to call the chopper back. A second helicopter, the first sign I'd seen of people since leaving the pad, appeared on the periscope screen.

I heard the hook catch hold in the top of the capsule. "O.K." the pilot radioed, "you've got two minutes to come out." By pre-arranged plan, if I didn't come out then, he would assume I wasn't going to and would carry me to the carrier inside the capsule. I asked him if he would please lift us a little higher. I could still see water out the window and didn't want the capsule to take a wave through the door when I opened it to get out and climb into the sling. He obligingly hoisted it up a foot or two. That looked better. I told him I'd be out in 30 seconds. I took off the helmet, disconnected the communications lead and took a last look around. This was a fine capsule and I was grateful. I opened the door and came on out, head first, looking up toward the chopper, reaching for the sling that would haul me up those last 25 feet.

## We'd Brought Off a Good One

Sitting in the chopper on the way back to the carrier, I felt relieved and happy. I knew I'd done a pretty good job and it had all worked out even better than we thought it would. The Mercury systems were good and I'd had a fine and effective ride. We'd brought off a good one, right out in the open where the whole world could watch us take our chances. I was feeling very chipper and was just about to start talking with the pilot on the intercom when we came up over the port side of the carrier. I looked down and saw a great press of people covering the after part of the deck, jammed in among the planes and packed all over the island. As we came in to set the capsule down on the cleared part of the deck I saw that all these people were being held back by the master-at-arms force and by ropes, that they were all looking up at the chopper and yelling. I remember thinking at this point, well, here are all these people yelling for me, and I thought of a lot of other men who deserved to share that moment with me. I had a great sense of gladness and humility.

A lot happened in the hours that passed before I was able to share the experiences of the flight with the other Astronauts. On the carrier I was given a careful medical examination, I talked the flight into a tape recorder and then I spoke by phone to the President. When I was finally taken to Grand Bahama Island for more debriefing, Deke Slayton and Gus Grissom were waiting. They had flown down from Cape Canaveral, and Gus had a little welcoming present for me. It was the box of crayons.

# Civil Rights Freedom Riders Are Attacked in the South

### By Helen Fuller

A 1955 law enacted by the U.S. Interstate Commerce Commission had banned segregation on interstate transportation carriers. More recently, in 1960, the Supreme Court had ruled in *Boynton v. Virginia* that racial segregation in interstate bus and rail terminals was unconstitutional. Some cities in the South, however, refused to follow the law and still permitted the segregation of passengers in bus stations and buses. In May 1961 members of the Congress of Racial Equality (CORE), a racially integrated civil rights group, traveled the South aboard public buses in a series of "Freedom Rides" to protest the continued segregation of black bus passengers.

After an initially peaceful journey, the Freedom Riders were physically attacked by angry white mobs in the Deep South state of Alabama. Helen Fuller describes in the following analysis how Alabama authorities denied the Freedom Riders police protection, despite promises to the U.S. attorney general Robert Kennedy that the mobs would be controlled. Fuller contends that President John F. Kennedy's administration must use its legal powers to enforce civil rights laws in states like Alabama and Mississippi, which operate in complete defi-

ance of the Supreme Court. Fuller worked as the Washington correspondent for the *New Republic* magazine during the 1960s.

"**W**hen the war between the states and the nation
ended," Civil War historian William B. Hessel-
tine points out, "the bodies of those who had died
that 'this nation, under God, shall not perish from the earth' rested
in neat rows in *national* cemeteries." Some forgetful Alabamans
recently had to be reminded how that contest came out. Painful
though the process was, it contained some "useful lessons for us
all to learn," as John F. Kennedy remarked about another recent
disaster. But as usual on such occasions eyewitnesses differ about
why the calamity occurred and what "lessons" it should teach.

## Freedom Riders Meet Southern Mobs

The story began on May 5 [1961] when 13 white and Negro men
and women, members of the Congress of Racial Equality
[CORE], left Washington, D.C., by bus. Purpose: to challenge
segregation in the buses and in the waiting rooms, rest rooms and
restaurants of bus stations between Washington and New Orleans. Calling themselves "Freedom Riders," the 13 progressed
with only minor incidents down through North and South Carolina, across Georgia and as far as the Alabama state line. But at
Anniston, Alabama, the mobile sit-in demonstrators met a mob
that beat them and set fire to their bus. (The bus is a significant
institution in the South. The poor man's transportation, it stops
right downtown where passengers mix and mingle as they would
not at an outlying railroad station.) Organized hoodlums again
hauled the riders off the substitute bus that carried them on to
Birmingham. No police help came, though the city hall was just
around the corner.

When bus drivers refused to haul the Freedom Riders on to
Montgomery for fear of further attacks, the group reluctantly
abandoned the bus and escaped to New Orleans and thence back
north to their homes by plane.

In spite of the change in plans, CORE headquarters and the riders, proud of their foray, were preparing a celebration in Washington when word came of a new development. Inspired by the
CORE riders, a group of students in the Nashville Non-Violence
Movement had resolved to join the CORE caravan. But by the

time seven of them reached Birmingham, the original party had gone. Determined to carry on, the Nashville group tried to board buses for Montgomery until taken into "protective custody" by the police and finally driven to the Tennessee state line and released. But the seven borrowed a car and drove back to Birmingham.

Meanwhile 12 more followers of the Martin Luther King [civil rights leader] version of passive resistance had arrived. A Department of Justice representative had tried to deter the reinforcements by pointing out to the 22-year-old organizer of the Nashville protest, Diane Nash, how dangerous the situation in Alabama had become.

"It was as if I were talking to a wall," the spokesman later told a reporter. "She never listened to a word." Miss Nash explained in her turn that there was no need to listen: "We aren't going to stop, not now. Why, those people in Alabama think they can ignore the President of the United States, and they think they can still win by beating us Negroes over the head."

"We saw this as a chance to go ahead and the kids wanted to go. All the kids knew that death was a real possibility on this trip. John Lewis [a student who had made the first part of the trip] told us how rough it was. Each kid who went said he was willing to give his life."

On Saturday, May 20 the Nashville group boarded a bus in Birmingham for Montgomery.

## Empty Promises of Protection

By this time, however, they were a quiet cause for official commotion. For five days following the refusal of bus drivers to transport the CORE riders to Montgomery, free travel had not been possible in Alabama. FBI reports on Birmingham and Montgomery and talks with leaders of the Freedom Riders made the Attorney General so apprehensive that he began to lay plans for swiftly assembling a large civilian force for an emergency. After Little Rock,[1] coming to understand what uniformed troops still symbolize to the Southern mind, Attorney General William P. Rogers had set up a special program of riot training for deputy federal marshals. Robert Kennedy gave orders to make them ready.

Meanwhile Kennedy was constantly on the telephone—re-

1. In 1957, Central High School in Little Rock, Arkansas, was desegregated, leading Governor Orval Faubus to call out the National Guard to prevent black students from entering.

peatedly calling [Alabama governor] John Patterson, police officials, bus owners and union representatives, trying to start the wheels rolling again. After days of getting no answer when he tried to reach Patterson, the Attorney General asked the President to try his luck—still no answer. A telegram from Patterson finally requested a Presidential representative to talk things over.

On the night of May 18, John Siegenthaler, aide to Robert Kennedy, received the Governor's pledge that he could and would fully protect everyone in Alabama under any contingency and his assurance that he needed no federal assistance to do it. Specifically, the Governor guaranteed the safe passage of the bus due to bring the Freedom Riders to Montgomery the next morning, discussing in detail with his aides the best way of doing so. Siegenthaler phoned Robert Kennedy from the Governor's office to report the agreement. And at Patterson's suggestion Justice officials notified the Greyhound Bus Company of the guarantee.

Up to a point it was carried out. State highway patrol officers flanked the bus all the way to the Montgomery city limits to prevent hijacking; a state-owned plane kept surveillance overhead. But at the city limits the protection ended. Not a single policeman was in sight when the bus drove in, although the FBI had notified the police department of the need for special protection.

The armed mob that was there, witnesses say, could have been any group of lower middle-class Southerners and their wives out for an outing. "There was a really gay atmosphere about the whole thing, like taking the children to a parade . . . their attitude was one of real jolliness and when one of the women would scream 'Go get him!', it was exactly the same yell you hear at football games."

When the President's representative, Mr. Siegenthaler, happening to drive by, tried to rescue a young girl being pursued by attackers, he was beaten unconscious for his trouble and police allowed him to lie in the street for nearly half an hour.

The next day, Sunday, some 400 deputy US marshals, led by Deputy Attorney General Byron White, and Martin Luther King, flanked by his veteran leaders from the "sit-in" campaigns, separately came to town. Before the day was out only the presence of the marshals had prevented an even larger and wilder mob from attacking a rally of the Reverend King's followers, and the Governor had admitted failure by declaring a state of martial law and summoning his Alabama National Guard to keep order. But the mob thought it had won when it surrounded the church, and still thought it had won the next morning. "None of the guys will get in jail, just wait and see."

Those Freedom Riders who did not land in the hospital hid out in private homes while the Reverend King, CORE leaders (who had hastily moved to rejoin the Ride) and Non-Violence leaders from around the country met to decide where to go from there.

Siegenthaler, dismissed from the Montgomery hospital after his head wounds were patched up, hurried back to Washington where Robert Kennedy was trying to anticipate the next guerrilla attack in the South.

## Hopes and Assumptions

No one expected just what happened in Montgomery. The Freedom Riders were "looking for trouble" in that they wanted to shatter any local law they could find that stood across the path of federally sanctioned civil rights. But they were not seeking broken heads or smoke bombs. The spontaneous decision of Nashville students to join an abandoned venture caught the cautious Non-Violence leaders temporarily off guard.

Far less bullish politicians than Robert and John F. Kennedy might have assumed that at some safe point they could reason with their strong backer for the 1960 Presidential nomination, John Patterson, to handle the bus matter their way, and could expect that in return for substantial patronage say-so as Democratic National Committeeman for Alabama, Birmingham Police Commissioner Eugene Connor might be willing to see a few things Washington's way.

Also a slow-thinking young Governor could not be blamed too much for assuming the loyalty of those associated with him when he had decided to give in to the Administration's demand for law enforcement. (There are knowledgeable insiders who attest that Patterson was dumbfounded when Commissioner Sullivan's police went AWOL and who attach significance to the fact that when Sullivan finally appeared at the bus station following the riot, he was in the company of Attorney General Gallion, candidate for Governor to succeed Patterson, and hopefully to take over his white supremacy following.) Nor was it foolish on the face of it for the Governor to hope that in time his demanding friends in Washington would stop phoning impossible demands and come to understand his need to leave office a "popular" man on the race issue if he was to have any future usefulness to them. After all, they had not been tough to get along with before.

There was no reason at all for Patterson to suppose either that major newspapers of the state would choose this moment to abandon him, but they did. *The Birmingham News*, the day after the second Montgomery riot, headlined an editorial across the top of page one: "We, the people, asked for it. As we wail in our anguish, let us not forget it. . . . We, the people, let the Governor of the great state of Alabama, John Patterson, talk for months in a manner that could easily say to the violent, the intemperate . . . that they were free to do as they pleased when it came to the 'hated' integrationists. We, the people, have let gangs of vicious men ride this state now for months. . . ." *The Montgomery Advertiser* declared that the measure of Patterson's errors was that "these Freedom Riders passed through every state from Washington to Alabama. But only Alabama . . . has a problem because of it."

The protests against tolerance of violence by these papers would have come with more grace and persuasiveness *before* their own reporters and photographers had been beaten. Alabama newspapers with few exceptions have stood rigidly defensive against articles in Northern newspapers and magazines which described the lawless situation in Birmingham. And when *The New Republic* (May 30, 1960) wrote of "the lack of legal restraints that exist today in Birmingham," the *Post-Herald* in that city replied (June 9) with the charge that we were guilty of "vicious misinformation."

## The Need for Federal Protection

Everyone involved encountered some element of the unexpected. Governor Patterson managed to convince himself he could have it both ways: take public credit with the redneck racists for refusing to "escort" the "agitators," and avoid physical clashes by jailing a few under special injunction. He misjudged the mood of a public after seven years of incitement to defiance of the Supreme Court by most of its elected officials, and overestimated his personal political skill.

The tardy action of the Governor in calling out units of the Alabama National Guard has quieted the scene momentarily, but what reason is there for faith in any basic improvement? The Guard, itself segregated, acts under orders from Patterson whose character has been exposed by the best authority—himself. Police Commissioners Connor and Sullivan of Birmingham and Montgomery have demonstrated minimum concern for lawful protection. The Attorney General of Alabama is a candidate for Governor and has his mind on votes. Any member of the Alabama delegation in Congress who spoke out just now against the mobs would be a dead duck in the next election. True, a hero among them would be acclaimed by the nation, but what about the Klansman who probably would take his place?

In short, no vehicle of substantial and immediate improvement is available within Alabama leadership. Indeed the short-time result of this initial federal intervention is likely to be negative. The toughs will be after more blood. The remaining liberals and moderates in Alabama today have been under pressure and suspicion, and now literally must be silent for their lives.

Under these circumstances, active federal concern for the protection of lives in Alabama, and probably in Mississippi, cannot in good sense be slacked off in the near future, and certainly not until officials of these two states have demonstrated a change of attitude.

In this connection, the full vigor of federal authority in tracking down and convicting the guilty leaders of the mobs can have a vastly sobering effect.

The President seems to be wisely reserving his personal influence against a larger crisis. But with his backing, Robert Kennedy acted in the Alabama incidents in a way to leave no room for questions as to his courage and resolution. To do this without bringing down a storm of condemnation from Southern Democrats in Congress speaks volumes for the relationships of the Kennedys with these men over the years.

The Attorney General also seems to have a proper measure of the difficulty ahead. "This is just one incident in a long struggle," the younger Kennedy said the morning after the Sunday violence. "It's going to continue not for weeks and months but for long into the future." With this prospect in mind, the Attorney General's office is proceeding at full speed to prepare for future troubles by locating and surrounding them. The FBI is fanning out over the South trying to spot potential outbreaks before they can happen. And Kennedy men are trying hard to keep lines of communication open to the direct action civil rights groups.

In building his strategy, Mr. Kennedy should not underestimate the fervor and force of the non-violent assault on Jim Crow.

"The moment has come," Martin Luther King told the embattled Negroes in the First Baptist Church after the riot was broken up, "for a full-scale—non-violent—massive assault on the system of segregation in the South." His colleague, the fiery Rev. Fred Shuttlesworth of Birmingham, put it less elegantly that same night: "Let's go on and get it all now . . . no more compromise." The 65,000 Negro college students who will begin summer vacations in a few days play an important part in these plans.

And we must hope that the Administration understands too that Alabama and Mississippi cannot at this stage be treated like North Carolina and Virginia. States which practice total defiance of the Supreme Court must be dealt with somewhat differently than states that have yielded somewhat. For Alabama, the visit of the Freedom Riders was a kind of extension of the Autherine Lucy[2] case. The state escaped facing its moment of truth then by raising the false issue of Miss Lucy's motives in seeking admission to the University of Alabama and by resorting to violence. If the Negroes persist boldly in claiming their rights and the federal government persists in protecting their persons while they do so, however, the moment will be near.

The Administration could speed it, if in addition to the use of his moral and legal powers, the President does not overlook the economic weapons in his hand. They might be the most effective of all. They could reach the sensitive perception of the conservative business community of the South which for the most part until now has remained, in appearance at least, above the howling strife. The business community of Montgomery would rock on its foundations should the federal government restrict activity at Maxwell Air Force Base, which provides much of Montgomery's daily bread as well as all of its butter.

In Alabama, as in most of the South, the lines of economic and political power run from elected officials in Birmingham and Montgomery straight to New York, Washington and other cities of the North. The belief is inescapable that if the men at the other end of those lines were to act with courage and in terms of the highest moral and national interest—or just because the Administration in Washington asked them to—they could improve things in Alabama.

2. On February 3, 1956, Autherine Lucy, a black woman, enrolled as a graduate student at the University of Alabama. Lucy was assaulted by white mobs and subsequently expelled by the school, ostensibly to protect her personal safety.

# Student Activism Increases on College Campuses

## By Jessica Mitford Treuhaft

Young Americans in the 1950s were dubbed the Silent Generation because of their tendency to accept the status quo and enjoy the nation's
unprecedented postwar prosperity. In the later years of the decade,
however, black college students led nonviolent protests against the entrenched racial segregation of the South, inspiring some of their white
peers to participate. By the summer of 1961, civil rights leader Martin
Luther King Jr. had noted the increasing activism of college students.
He asserted that the black student movement had led to a "revival of
social awareness . . . across [college] campuses from Cambridge to
California," and had "spilled over the boundaries of the single issue of
desegregation and encompassed questions of peace, civil liberties, capital punishment, and others."

   As a young journalist, Jessica Mitford Treuhaft commented exten-
sively on the burgeoning student movement for several West Coast
newspapers in the early 1960s. In the following essay, she chronicles
the rise of political activism at the University of California, Berkeley,
beginning in the late 1950s. According to Treuhaft, the current generation of students has moved away from apathy and conformity and become "issue-oriented," forming political groups to fight social injustice. She argues that having experienced some success in their

Jessica Mitford Treuhaft, "The Indignant Generation . . . ," *The Nation*, vol. 192, May 27, 1961,
pp. 451–56. Copyright © 1961 by The Nation Company, Inc. Reproduced by permission.

activism, it is unlikely that the students' newly awakened concern for social causes will lose momentum in the years ahead.

**"T**he employers will love this generation, they are not going to press many grievances. . . . They are going to be easy to handle. There aren't going to be any riots." Buried somewhere in a 1959 publication of the American Council on Education reporting a conference on the college student, this prophecy by Clark Kerr, President of the University of California, today has a curiously outdated ring. A few scattered signposts on a number of campuses, including his own, might even then have suggested a qualification of this flat judgment; in any event, shortly before Commencement of the following year, San Francisco Bay Area newspapers exploded with the news, STUDENTS RIOT AT HOUSE UN-AMERICAN COMMITTEE HEARING.[1] Of the fourteen hospitalized and sixty-odd arrested that day and the thousands who subsequently demonstrated against the committee (the *San Francisco Chronicle* estimated 5,000), the majority were from the University of California's Berkeley campus.

## Abandoning Apathy and Conformity

In the welter of charges and countercharges, praise and censure that followed, one fact emerged: the current crop of students had gone far to shake the label of apathy and conformity that had stuck through the fifties. What started this campus dynamism? Did it herald the development of a genuine student movement?

Any exploration of trends among students must first be hedged with some obvious qualifications. The University of California students who have been making headlines are a small minority of the 21,800 gestating in the capacious womb of that vast alma mater. The amount of support that the minority is able to muster fluctuates widely, depending on the issue. The student community and its organizations are by their nature in a constant state of change; not only is there a total turnover every few years, but each individual youngster is at a unique time of life, undergoing his own particular metamorphosis from adolescence to adulthood. Generalizations about the political views held by students are particularly fraught with the danger of over-simplification,

---

1. The HUAC was a congressional committee formed in 1937 to investigate subversive activities by Americans.

for students, in this area as in others, are the most prone to change in a changing world.

Nevertheless, there is a continuity, however tenuous it may appear. Each campus has its internal history, shaped to a large extent by surrounding circumstances and developing within the context of its particular locale. Trends at the University of California are mirrored in varying degrees elsewhere in the country.

## Subdued Activism in the Postwar Years

The tradition of student radicalism, in California as elsewhere at its strongest in the thirties, was maintained at best sporadically with the coming of World War II. Student life and its political aspects were disrupted and obscured during the war years. A brief postwar flare-up of activity around Henry Wallace's 1948 campaign for the Presidency soon subsided, and for almost ten years was followed by an eerie, unyouthful silence that gave some of the older generation the creeps.

Nevertheless, many faculty members, long familiar with the genus student, believe that they never were as uniformly passive as generally believed. Professor Nevitt Sanford of the Psychology Department pointed out that it was convenient for many years to lump the students together as "cautious, passive, indifferent." Actually, he recalled, in 1950, the year of the University of California loyalty oath, 5,000 undergraduate signatures were obtained in support of the non-signing professors. The head of steam that was generated over this issue was dissipated not so much by "student apathy" as by the unseemly capitulation of some of their elders. Thus a professor vowed to a mass meeting of students that never, as long as he lived, would he sign the despicable oath—or any similar oath; the following week he meekly threw in the sponge and signed.

The years immediately following imposition of the loyalty oath saw considerable disruption of the university, an emigration to other institutions by many liberal faculty leaders, and a corresponding exodus of their students. Dr. Leonard Wolf of the English Department at San Francisco State College, who was an undergraduate at U.C. at the time, recalls: "The university suffered generally from a clobbered feeling. The apathy came down from above. As somebody said of the faculty and students of those days, 'It was a case of the bland leading the bland.'"

A factor that contributed to damping down any form of political high jinks during those years was the enormous enrollment, up until the late fifties, of service veterans. "The Korean War produced many more vets than you'd think," said Henry Mash Smith, Chairman of the English Department. "These fellows figured they'd already lost a few years out of their lives, and all they wanted was peace and quiet, time to catch up. A lot of them were married men with family responsibilities. Today, for the first time in years, we're seeing a generation of youngsters who have what we might term 'normal' youthful reactions to the world around them."

After the losing battle over the loyalty oath, holding operations of sorts persisted at the University of California, despite the distinctly unfavorable political climate of the McCarthy period.[2] Such activity as there was revolved around Stiles Hall, the campus YMCA, which became an informal meeting place for campus liberals. There were Students to Combat McCarthyism and various social action committees for peace and civil rights—evidence that the liberal spirit never quite died out.

## A New Sense of Urgency

It was not until 1957—coincidentally the year of McCarthy's death—that any sign of "normal youthful reactions" appeared. The stated issue was "a meaningful alternative to the *status quo*"; the vehicle, a crusading political party called SLATE.

The story of how SLATE came into being is told in the now yellowing pages of 1957–58 editions of the *Daily Californian* [student newspaper], minutes of meetings of those days and copies of mimeographed leaflets once distributed in the thousands. These documents still breathe with the freshness and sense of urgency that mark a cause undertaken with great conviction and high hopes. In the fall elections of 1957, six students formed a slate (hence the name of the organization) pledged to combat what they called "sandbox politics"—a derisive reference to the limited activities of the entrenched student government—and to fight for student participation in national and international affairs. They adopted electoral tactics in keeping with their militant program; for the first time in years, leaflets, petitions, open-air mass meetings were introduced on campus, and the election

2. Senator Joseph McCarthy led an anti-Communist witch-hunt against his political adversaries in the early 1950s.

took place in a storm of controversy. The slate went down to electoral defeat, but when all the smoke had cleared away, it was evident they could chalk up some significant accomplishments. The *Daily Californian*, which had raged against the six insurgents editorially, summed it up. "We have often, in print, disagreed with . . . SLATE and the way they go about things. In fact, we still disagree with them. But we must give SLATE some credit—they have turned this into a real election in which real issues are being debated." The unprecedented interest in the election was reflected in a total vote almost twice as large as usual, of which SLATE candidates received 35–40 per cent.

The ebb and flow of SLATE's fortunes in subsequent years are pretty typical of such organizations. Its dues-paying nucleus remained tiny—from 150 to 200. Yet its effectiveness as gadfly, pricking into the open issues long smothered under indifference, was considerable, and far out of proportion to its actual numerical strength. Action committees, some affiliated with SLATE and some independent, sprang into being. Students for Civil Liberties, Students for Racial Equality, Utopians for Political Action. From time to time, although infrequently, SLATE candidates were elected to office—on one occasion to the presidency of the student government. The *Daily Californian* reflected these developments; from being a relatively dull publication reporting the usual campus social and sports events, it became a turbulent forum for thrashing out issues and tactics.

No doubt the great majority of students remained unmoved by SLATE's activities, and many were hostile. Yet its vociferous and insistent presence on campus did contribute to a new interest in minority viewpoints, a new tolerance for unorthodoxy. This was vividly demonstrated by student reaction to the surprisingly effective one-man hunger strike staged in the fall of 1959 by Fred Moore, a freshman, son of a Virginia colonel, against compulsory ROTC [Reserve Officers Training Corps]. Some 7,000 signatures supporting Moore's position were gathered on the Berkeley and Los Angeles campuses of the university.

## From Polite Protest to Direct Action

Events of early 1960 added a new dimension to the growing student desire to do something about the problems of the world. The example of student militancy elsewhere—Korea, Japan, the Middle East—had an impact. More important, the student conscience was deeply stirred by two events closer to home which, as one expressed it, "illuminate the hollow cynicism of the prevailing morality": the agonizing cat-and-mouse proceedings which led to Caryl Chessman's execution [a California man whose execution in May 1960 generated protests], and the Southern sit-ins. It was on these issues that students moved over from polite protest by petition into direct action—the "non-violent direct action" that was to become their hallmark. Hundreds of California students embraced Chessman's cause as their own, demonstrating in a series of all-night vigils outside San Quentin's walls. The sit-in movement—with its clear-cut goals and the simplicity of the Negro students' form of protest—had an impact the strength of which is hard to measure. University of California students were among the first of Northern college groups (now estimated at over 130) to dash into action with a supporting picket line organized by the Congress of Racial Equality around the Berkeley Woolworth's.

With several hundred students already involved in various sorts of political protests, it is hardly surprising that they swung around to meet a new challenge when an eighteen-year-old University of California sophomore and a number of local school

*Student demonstrators at the University of California at Berkeley followed the principles of non-violence established by the Southern sit-ins.*

teachers were among those subpoenaed for the 1960 hearing of the House Committee on Un-American Activities. (The HUAC was already in unusually hot water in the Bay Area, for the year before it had subpoenaed 110 California school teachers for a hearing on "communism in education," only to call it off in the face of unprecedented community opposition.)

The people under subpoena were an odd miscellany, including Communist Party leaders, housewives, workers, lawyers, teachers—a mixed bag. In any event, for the students organizing the protest line, the question of whether those subpoenaed were or were not Communists was supremely beside the point. As they saw it, here was one more "moral issue" to be joined, this time involving the right of a Congressional committee to swoop down upon assorted John Does and grill them about their political views.

Two weeks before the hearings, SLATE called an informal meeting on campus, attended by fifty students, to map the form of protest: a picket line and demonstration outside San Francisco's City Hall. Demonstrators were asked to follow principles established by the Southern sit-ins: non-violence, strict obedience to orders of the monitors, no retorts to provocation by hecklers. From that first meeting, interest mushroomed, given an able assist by many faculty members who welcomed this new concern with national issues. Within days, 2,000 signatures were collected at the university on a petition calling for cancellation of the hearings and abolition of HUAC; liberal groups on other campuses were alerted to join the picket line; an Episcopal canon and two state assemblymen agreed to address the demonstration; the *Daily Californian* exhorted its readers to attend the hearings.

The majority of the 1,000 students who flocked to San Francisco's City Hall on the first two days of the hearings were more or less antagonistic to the committee. But many others came out of curiosity. There was by no means uniform hostility toward the committee, nor uniform sympathy for the witnesses.

## Vanishing Neutrality

At the moment of the clash with police something changed, and the results of that change aré likely to be evident among the students for a long time to come.

It must be remembered that several hundred were soaked to the skin, dragged or shoved bodily down a long flight of steps, and that in the indiscriminate hosing, clubbings and arrests that followed many neutral observers were swept up. In the course of this, all neutrality vanished, to be replaced with a hot, sustained anger still evident in those who witnessed the events. One of the merely curious who was hosed and arrested and returned the next day to join the protest commented ruefully, "I was a political virgin, but I was raped on the steps of City Hall."

A choosing-up of sides in the community at large was inevitable and immediate. Bay Area newspapers, even those that had opposed the hearings, on the whole chastised the students for rowdy behavior. People closer to the picture tended to support the rebellious students. Eighty-four Stanford professors expressed a view widely held in faculty circles throughout the area: "Our understanding of the evidence leads us to declare that, contrary to a wide misinterpretation in the press, the demonstration was for the most part a responsible protest by mature college students against what they deeply felt to be the committee's intolerable infringement on civil freedom." Most liberals applauded—with reservations. The *East Bay Labor Journal*, organ of the AFL-CIO, editorialized, "We feel that this re-awakening is a good thing," but warned, "we may be sure that the Commies will take advantage of the new swing to politics on the campus. When they do, it will be time to blow the whistle."

Two months after the event, during the summer vacation, J. Edgar Hoover [director of the FBI from 1924 to 1972] blew the whistle long and loud in an eighteen-page illustrated report, published by the HUAC, in which he ascribed the City Hall fracas to Communist infiltration and agitation tactics: "Communist leaders in Berkeley arranged transportation from Berkeley to San Francisco for youths interested in attending each of the three-day hearings," and "placards and posters were also prepared for the demonstrators to carry." The report added: "Particularly pleasing to party officials was the number of students involved in the demonstrations. They commented that there had not been that much 'political activity' among student groups for years."

While that last sentence is hardly debatable, Hoover's main thesis—that those involved were dupes "totally unaware of the extent to which they can be victimized and exploited by Communists"—brought forth astonished and furious denials from the students, and caused considerable eyebrow lifting on the part of faculty members.

The chairman of the University of California Students for Civil

Liberties issued a sharp denial of Hoover's charges, declaring that statements inferring Communist infiltration of the student movement were "nothing more than hogwash." Unkindest cut of all to the students was that Communist agitators should be credited with the carefully planned demonstration held the last day of the hearing. "Of course there were Communists at City Hall—a lot of them were subpoenaed by the committee," said a student in a burst of irritation. "But what's that got to do with us? We *know* who arranged for transportation, who made the placards, who were picket captains—because *we* did it.". . .

## Working to Change the *Status Quo*

To predict the next development on the student front would be hazardous. But one can, at least, make some pertinent generalizations concerning today's student movement.

First of all, it is essentially non-political. Its main philosophical current is in the tradition of the Quakers, the Rev. Martin Luther King, Jr., and Gandhi rather than that of Karl Marx and the class struggle. There is a scattering of Socialists (the Young Peoples Socialist League claims some thirty members at the University of California), but no organization, either open or secret, of Communists. (Interestingly, student after student, asked to estimate the strength of the Communist Party on campus, replied that it was non-existent.)

A minor influence was exerted for a time by the Beat Generation [a 1950s countercultural movement inspired by a group of poets and novelists]. A number of politically active students admit to past flirtation with beat ideas. They point out that the beat insistence on the futility of trying to improve the world is in a sense the other side of the coin to action, since both stem from the same deep disillusionment with the *status quo*. But as a University of California graduate student said, "The minute you join a picket line or circulate a petition you're not 'beat' any more, because you're actually working for something you believe in."

The beats may have helped crystallize for the students a concept of what they are *against*. A list of pet phobias, compiled from conversations with a number of students, have a beat ring: "Specious ideas . . . sacred cows of American life . . . institutions [like the FBI, House Un-American Activities Committee] that represent themselves as above criticism . . . compromisers . . . the Madison Avenue mentality. . . ."

But what are "the vocal minority of rebels" *for*? To the question, "What would you say is the guiding philosophy of the active student movement?" a twenty-three-year-old University of California English major replied, "The student movement is based on very general principles for rights, justice and so on. Many of us are for things that no political party has come out for—most of us are for banning the bomb. We just work on a broad set of principles, and as issues come up, we decide how to act. We approach all the problems without the strict theory that older people are so fond of."

## Thinking for Themselves

It is this aspect of the student movement that is truly new, and which differentiates it most sharply from its predecessors of the thirties and forties. Students today are not so much *political* as *moral*. They are *for* the simple, liberal issues—free speech, civil rights, ending the nuclear threat. Above all, they intend to provide their own leadership, and they look with jaundiced eye on most adult organizations: political parties, which they see as riddled with opportunism; the labor movement, which they consider badly compromised; the remnants of left-wing organizations, which they consider hide-bound, restrictive of thought, and prone to pat solutions.

The world around them has changed; gone are the virile Left-led movements of the thirties, with their highly disciplined youth branches. The very language of today's students reflects the change. They talk in different terms because they *think* in different terms. The "politically developed forces" of yesteryear have been replaced by the "emotionally committed." Little is heard about "ideological struggle," for today's students are, as they say, "issue-oriented"—a phrase which crops up over and over again in their gatherings and publications. Rather than of a "united front" with racial minorities, etc., they speak of "moral identity." The words "concerned" and "dedicated," with their connotations of humanistic solicitude, and that meaningless word "meaningful," sprinkle student conversation.

The wariness of existing ideologies may be better understood if one first understands what it is that today's students do *not* fear. The danger of being "smeared" by association with left-wing groups, or being "labeled" as radical, is not uppermost in their minds. It is rather that they are shy of the *content* of existing left-wing organizations and ideologies. They strongly desire to think things through for themselves.

## Handling Charges of Communism

There are, however, increasing signs that the purely "issue oriented" approach may be in for some overhauling. If the City Hall affair was for hundreds of students the first time they (literally) got their feet wet in political action, the totally unexpected charges of "red infiltration" drew new battle lines and created new complexities. Now they find themselves directly under the gun—victims rather than defenders —with a host of morning-after headaches that cannot be resolved by merely pointing to inaccuracies in the Hoover report and the film [*Operation Abolition*, made from footage of the 1960 HUAC hearing in San Francisco].

What should be their posture regarding the charges of communism? A strong sentiment for an "anti-Communist disclaimer" among liberal faculty advisers and students is matched by an equally strong sentiment against such a step. The argument for it is persuasive: since the student leaders are not Communists, and in fact disagree with the Communist Party, its tactics, method of organization, and its economic and political conclusions, why not say so and avoid this particular stigma? Opponents of the disclaimer see the issue as one of political expediency versus principle. They say it's one thing to disagree privately with the Communists, but to disavow them publicly is to lend aid and comfort to the witch-hunt. Why capitulate on this point and institute what would amount to a loyalty oath within the student movement, the very thing students have opposed? Who knows if such an oath, even if adopted, would satisfy the HUAC—doesn't the committee's past history show that the only people it considers "pure" of Communist leanings are those willing to testify against their co-workers?

## Looking Toward the Future

There is also the question of what form the student movement should take, and which way it should go. Here, the posed alternatives (so familiar to older hats in radical movements, but so brand new and challenging to today's students) are between the broad appeal to the middle-of-the-road majority, and the quick response to issues by a small, dedicated band of militants willing to act quickly find dramatically. Should the movement seek radical changes in our society, or content itself with meeting specific issues—racial bigotry, civil liberty, etc.—as they arise?

Many students are seriously plagued with the necessity of deciding what to do and where to go after leaving school. They see no parallel to the student movement outside campus walls. Most liberal adult organizations devoted to the cause of peace and civil liberties are composed of people middle-aged and older, and have little appeal to the recent college graduate. The world of jobs and careers seems tainted with all the evils of the affluent society, an unattractive place to land from the high-minded, strongly idealistic life of the student movement. Some are solving this problem by simply staying on at college, not as the academically immured "perennial student" but as dedicated workers in what they regard as the only "live" movement for progress presently in existence.

While the students are acutely aware of the difficulties confronting them, they also have a strong feeling of achievement; they have already had an impact on national life. They have seen both major political conventions give official praise and recognition to the Southern sit-ins. Their attack on the HUAC has had country-wide repercussions. Their walks for peace have been headlined in papers from coast to coast.

Their mood is one of youthful indignation and muscle flexing. There is a desire to become re-connected with society and to play an influential part in shaping the future of the world. Whether or not the student organizational drive is sustained at its present rate, the thinking of young people has been touched and transformed in a significant new way. It is unlikely that those students who have espoused new causes, and have begun to taste the sweet fruits of success in their efforts, will subside into silence.

# Cold War Ideologies Clash at the Vienna Summit

By *U.S. News & World Report*

On June 3 and 4, 1961, President Kennedy met with Soviet premier Nikita S. Khrushchev in Vienna, Austria, seeking diplomatic solutions to several conflicts that had brought Cold War tensions to a dangerous crescendo. Foremost on President Kennedy's agenda was the dispute over Berlin, the former capital of Germany, which had been divided into a Soviet-controlled eastern zone and a western zone occupied by the United States, Britain, and France (Western Allies) following World War II. Khrushchev was demanding that the Western Allies withdraw all military forces from West Berlin. Because the city was 110 miles within Soviet-ruled East Germany, an Allied withdrawal would consign more than 2 million West Berliners to life behind the Iron Curtain and forestall indefinitely the reunification of Germany.

The Southeast Asian nation of Laos was another area of disagreement. It had been engulfed in a civil war between Soviet-supported Communist rebels and a U.S.-backed, pro-American faction since its recent independence from France. The fall of Laos to Communist rule would hinder Kennedy's fight against communism in the region. At Vienna, Kennedy asked Khrushchev to continue the current cease-fire and endorse an independent Laos.

In the following analysis, the editors of the weekly newsmagazine

"Did Khrushchev Win at Vienna?" *U.S. News & World Report*, vol. 50, June 19, 1961, pp. 37–39.

*U.S. News & World Report* describe the "somber" atmosphere of the talks. Little substantive progress was made on Berlin, Laos, and other important issues such as nuclear disarmament and the growing Soviet support for Cuba. According to the authors, Khrushchev considered himself the "winner" of the summit for having refused to offer Kennedy any diplomatic concessions.

Out of the meeting of John F. Kennedy and Nikita S. Khrushchev in Vienna on June 3 and 4 has come this question:

Has Khrushchev emerged the winner?

Attitudes and actions on both sides immediately after the meeting suggested that the answer was "Yes."

## A "Somber" Outcome

Khrushchev cavorted and clowned at a Moscow diplomatic party on June 6, acting like a winner. Mr. Kennedy, through his aides and in an address to the American people that same day, used one word to describe the outlook for the U.S. That word was "somber."

Military action in Laos also indicated that Khrushchev had been the winner at Vienna. At dawn on June 7, Communist-led forces blasted away a cease-fire in the jungle kingdom of Laos with shot and shell, seizing the mile-high hamlet of Padong. The U.S., still hoping for a settlement, showed its disgust with Communists' broken promises by boycotting the Laos talks in Geneva, but agreed to return if the Reds quit shooting.

Yet, behind the contrasts of gaiety in Moscow and grimness in Washington, behind the shooting in Laos, the deadlock in Geneva, there was an air of mystery, a sense of change.

To seek out the facts and the trends to follow the Vienna meeting, *U.S. News & World Report* asked key questions of informed sources in Washington, London, Paris, Bonn and elsewhere.

The situation as it emerged in the answers to these questions:

*Over-all.* Talks at Vienna were mere preliminaries for the Big Two. Sooner or later, though both sides now are playing down the idea, there will be more talks between the two leaders in Vienna, Moscow or elsewhere.

In the meantime . . .

Words spoken by both leaders at Vienna are coming up for

testing in the battlefields of the cold war. Shooting in Laos was but one test, launched by Khrushchev. There will be others, at places and times chosen by Khrushchev, perhaps at places and times chosen by Mr. Kennedy.

## Trouble in Berlin and Laos

*Berlin.* "Our most somber talks," said Mr. Kennedy in his report to the American people, "were on the subject of Germany and Berlin."

On the surface there was deadlock on Berlin. Kennedy set out flatly that the U.S. would go to any length to protect its legal position in Berlin. And Khrushchev set out, in effect, that he would take steps to get his way in Berlin, leaving it up to U.S. to start a war. What Khrushchev wants is a demilitarized "free city" of Berlin which would really cloak a Red take-over, since the city is deep inside Communist East Germany.

What appears to be a deadlock on Berlin does in fact leave room for one or more "crises short of war," as Western diplomats see it. These crises may begin this autumn, if not before.

On June 8, Russia protested formally to the U.S. and its allies over plans to hold meetings of the West German Parliament in West Berlin this month. Such meetings, said the Soviet notes, constituted "a new major provocation."

Thus "heating up" the Berlin crisis, Khrushchev may demand a "peace conference" and there ask the U.S. to recognize "two Germanys"—East and West. A U.S. refusal would lead Khrushchev to sign a "separate peace" with his East German Communists, giving them "control" over Berlin's access routes.

Real testing time for the U.S. will come when East German Reds get Moscow's orders to bar Berlin to the West. Looking ahead, Mr. Kennedy told the Soviet boss that Russia, not the East Germans, will be held responsible for any attempt to close the routes to Berlin.

Khrushchev's answer to that statement at Vienna was, in effect: "So what?" Still to be tested, as Khrushchev sees it, is U.S. willingness to use guns, not just words, to go into West Berlin.

*Laos.* By June 8, the day after Communist guns had blasted at the hoped-for cease-fire in the Laotian civil war, U.S. officials were already swallowing this violation of the cease-fire. The capture of Padong by rebels, they said, was "merely a loss of real estate" without great tactical importance.

Said Prince Boun Oum, the anti-Communist leader whose Government once had full U.S. support: "Communist rebels march forward, shooting. It is not permitted to shoot at them because there is a cease-fire. Nothing can stop them. In three months we shall all be Communists, that's certain. And the whole world is an accomplice."

Yet President Kennedy himself had declared after Vienna that Laos was "the one area which afforded some immediate hope of accord." Khrushchev, said Kennedy, had endorsed the concept of a neutral and independent Laos, the importance of an effective cease-fire.

In terms of the war in Laos, thus, the Soviet dictator appeared to have emerged the winner of the Vienna talks by the time-tried Soviet method of promising one thing, doing another.

## Looming Threats

*Nuclear-test ban.* There was no sign Khrushchev had eased his stand on the nuclear-test-ban talks in Geneva.

On the contrary, Kennedy quietly offered a new concession to Khrushchev on the very eve of the Vienna talks in the hope of progress on the test-ban question. U.S. and Britain, which once had demanded a minimum number of 20 inspections on the spot in the Soviet Union each year under any test-ban agreement, suddenly offered to accept a minimum of 12 such inspections. This offer was made on May 29 through U.S. delegates at Geneva, but was rejected by Khrushchev's man the same day.

And, at Vienna, Khrushchev flatly called any inspection "only a subterfuge for espionage." Test-ban talks, the Soviet dictator said, "appeared futile."

On that point, too, Khrushchev appeared to have wrested a concession, giving no concession in return.

*Cuba.* At one point in the Vienna conversations, according to U.S. congressional leaders who got a special report from Mr. Kennedy, Cuba was discussed. Khrushchev indicated he considered Fidel Castro unstable and not a Communist. But, he told President Kennedy, "You are well on the way to making him a good one."

At this time Khrushchev is busily nailing down his Communist base in Castro's Cuba. European businessmen in Cuba report a steady movement of Soviet freighters in and out of Havana harbor, a steady flow of Russians, Chinese, other Communists into Cuba. What, if any, warning the U.S. President gave on Cuba has not been disclosed.

*Wars.* In the free-wheeling Vienna talks, as congressional leaders report the Kennedy version, the Big Two also got into the general subject of war. It was not made clear whether Khrushchev or Kennedy brought up this subject.

Khrushchev is reported to have said there were three kinds of war. He predicted that there will never be a nuclear war, thus indicating his conviction that the U.S. would never be the first to use nuclear weapons, and that Russia could win without using nuclear weapons. If it comes to conventional war, Khrushchev said, "We will put five divisions where you put only one."

Third kind of war, said Khrushchev, was the war of peoples seeking to overthrow tyrannical governments. In such wars, he said, Soviet support goes to the peoples against such governments.

## Courting Allies, Stirring Up Trouble

*Eastern Europe.* Perhaps in answer to Khrushchev's comment about Communist support for peoples against tyranny, Mr. Kennedy suggested that it might be a good idea to have free elections in Communist Poland.

This Kennedy comment drew Khrushchev's open anger for the first and only time in the Vienna talks. As Kennedy reported the incident to U.S. congressional leaders, Khrushchev flared with the comment that what happened in Poland was none of Mr. Kennedy's business.

By this single reference to one of the countries of the Communist empire, the U.S. President had touched the Soviet boss on a tender spot. Mr. Kennedy did not pursue the matter, but the U.S. warning was clear.

In recent years the Soviet boss has taken full advantage of his Communists, using them continuously to stir up trouble and revolt everywhere in the non-Communist world. If Khrushchev should press his "third kind of war" into other countries such as Cuba, then the U.S. and its allies may take a new look at the chances of stirring up trouble for Khrushchev among the oppressed peoples of Eastern Europe.

Another straw also was set whirling in the winds of change stirring about the Vienna meeting. Kennedy reported to the American people that Khrushchev said "no one was truly neutral." This was in connection with the demands Khrushchev made for a Soviet veto over all negotiations involving "neutral" third powers.

In Cairo, where President Gamal Abdel Nasser was playing host to a "neutralist conference" of other Governments, there was a sharp reaction, an open criticism of Soviet propaganda and interference with neutrals.

U.S., which once was wary of "neutrals," now courted them. And Khrushchev, who once courted "neutrals," now appeared to be expressing contempt for them. This was a switch.

Adding up the facts now learned about the Vienna Big Two talks. . . .

Khrushchev has taken the attitudes and risked the actions of a winner, while Kennedy has insisted that nothing was lost and something may have been gained for the U.S. at Vienna.

The months ahead, when the words of both the Western and Soviet leaders will be tested in more crises, more cold war, will provide proofs of which side really "won" at Vienna.

# Writer Ernest Hemingway Commits Suicide

## By Archibald MacLeish

On July 2, 1961, American author Ernest Hemingway died of a self-inflicted gunshot wound at his home in Ketchum, Idaho. Hemingway became something of an American icon during the 1930s and 1940s, famous both for his macho, larger-than-life persona and his unique writing style, which presented dialogue and descriptions with lean clarity. In short stories and novels such as *The Sun Also Rises* (1926) and *For Whom the Bell Tolls* (1940), Hemingway largely fictionalized his real-life adventures as a war correspondent during the Spanish Civil War and World War II and his travels in Africa.

Archibald MacLeish contends in the following remembrance that unlike many writers, Hemingway chose to actively participate in life rather than spend his time merely observing history and mankind. The result was that he became a "poet of the human experience," recording events as he "really" experienced them both physically and emotionally. In MacLeish's opinion, this unique approach to writing stands as Hemingway's great contribution to literature. MacLeish was a friend and contemporary of Hemingway, renowned for his Pulitzer Prize–winning poem *Conquistador.* He died in 1982.

Archibald MacLeish, "His Mirror Was Danger," *Life*, vol. 51, July 14, 1961, p. 71. Copyright © 1961 by Time, Inc. Reproduced by permission.

**I** wrote a poem some years ago in which there was a question about Hemingway and an answer:

. . . the lad in the Rue de Notre Dame des Champs
In the carpenter's loft on the left-hand side going down—
The lad with the supple look like a sleepy panther—
And what became of him? Fame became of him.
Veteran out of the wars before he was twenty:
Famous at twenty-five: thirty a master—
Whittled a style for his time from a walnut stick
In a carpenter's loft in a street of that April city.

Now, with his death, the question asks itself again: what became of him?

How shall that question be answered now? By the fame still? I don't suppose any writer since Byron has been as famous as Hemingway was when he died, but fame is a young man's passion. It has little to say to the fact of death.

Or is the style the answer? The style remains as surely as the fame. It has been praised, imitated and derided for 30 years, but it endures: the one intrinsic style our century has produced. And yet Hemingway was the last man to wish to be remembered as a stylist, and none of his critics, however much he has admired the style or detested it, has been able or willing to leave his judgment at that.

## Taking Part in Life

To answer one must go further back. It is not Hemingway's death or even the manner of his death which poses the question now: it is his life—the fact that his life is over and demands to be looked at, to be measured. What makes the answer difficult is that Hemingway's life was a strange life for a writer, as we think of writers in our time. Writers with us are supposed to be watchers: "God's spies" as John Keats [English Romantic poet] put it once. They are supposed to spend themselves observing the world, watching history and mankind and themselves—particularly themselves: their unsaid thoughts, their secret deeds and dreads. Hemingway was not a watcher; he was an actor in his life. He took part. What he took part in was not the private history of Ernest Hemingway or the social history of Oak Park, Illinois [Hemingway's hometown] or the intellectual history of a generation of his fellow countrymen. What he took part in was a public—even a universal—history of wars and animals and gigantic fish. And he did take part. He could never go to a war—and he went to every war available to him—without engaging in it. He went to the First World War as an ambulance driver and got his knee smashed by a shell in a front-line trench where no one had sent him. He went to the war in Spain to write a scenario for a movie and learned how you washed the powder burns off your hands without water. He went to the last World War as a correspondent—and worried the high command by turning up with other tools than typewriters—mementos he called them. And between wars there were lions and elephants. And between elephants and lions there were marlin. Also bears.

Again, modern writers, if you can believe the novels, associate with other writers or with other writers' wives or with the people

*Ernest Hemingway became famous during the 1930s and 1940s for his larger-than-life persona and unique writing style.*

who hang around writers. Hemingway preferred boxers and bicycle racers in Paris, and Charlie Thompson, and Old Bra in Key West, and nightclub addicts in New York and matadors in Spain and commercial fishermen and game-cock fighters in Cuba. He had writer friends. Scott Fitzgerald was a good friend, and [John] Dos Passos sometimes was and sometimes wasn't. But writers as writers—writers disguised as writers—he didn't fancy. He and I had lunch in the middle '20s with Wyndham Lewis, the painter who set himself up briefly and locally as a literary dictator in London. When the two of us walked off home across the river, Hemingway astonished me by saying, "Did you notice? He ate with his gloves on." He had too—though there were no gloves.

Most modern writers are literary—more so than ever now that the critical mind has completed its conquest—but Hemingway wasn't literary. He read as much as most English professors and he remembered what he read, remembered it usefully, and in its relevance to himself—but he rarely talked about writing. Ezra Pound, the greatest and most successful teacher of writing in our time, gave him up. "The son of a bitch's *instincts* are right," said Pound. But you can't converse about instincts. Even [André] Gide, the most articulate writer about writing in modern France, was defeated by that hulking body and artless air and charming smile. I had dragged Hemingway along to a French literary afternoon where Gide and Jules Romains and others of that generation sat on stiff-backed chairs around a bookshop wall talking as though they had rehearsed all morning, but Hemingway, whom all of them were watching, watched the floor. It was too much for Gide. He dropped the topic, whatever it was, and drew Hemingway aside to explain how he punished his cat. He punished his cat, he said, by lifting him up by the scruff of his neck and saying PHT! in his face. Whether Hemingway restrained a desire to hit him, I don't know. I was watching the back of his head.

## Derision and Admiration

A strange life for a writer and a difficult life to judge at the end. Indeed, a difficult life to judge before the end—which is perhaps why Hemingway attracted, alive, more critics of more schools and opinions than most writers who have been dead for centuries. Writers generally are judged by their work, but Hemingway's life kept threatening to get in the way of his work with the result that his critics never found themselves in agreement. Those who were drawn to him called him, as one of them actually did on the day of his death, "a man who lived it up to write it down." Those who were repelled—and most of the hostile critics seemed to have been repelled emotionally as well as intellectually—called him in one form of words or another a phony: a man who ran away from his real task to masquerade as a big game hunter or a hero or a tough guy. What they will say now I don't know—perhaps that he had run as far as he could and that the truth caught up with him at 7:30 on the morning of the second of July.

Both views are based on a misconception of the relation between a writer's task and a writer's life. Both conceive of life and writing as different and even contradictory things. The deploring critic thinks of Hemingway's life as a betrayal of his obligations: you don't fight marlin by the hour and watch the killing of 1,500 bulls if you are loyal to your writer's obligation to your craft. The admiring critic thinks of the obligation as incidental to the life: you shoot grizzlies and then you write about it. Neither understands the simple and primary fact that a writing—a true writing—is not the natural by-product of an isolated experience, nor the autonomous creation of an isolated man, but the consequence of a collision between the two. Neither realizes that the collision when it occurs, even when the experience is a lion in the gun sights or a German in a Normandy hedge, may provide, for the right writer, something more than a thrill and something very different from an escape. It may, indeed, provide a realization—precisely such a realization as the art of letters at its greatest is capable of providing: the realization of the meaning of a man. Danger is not the least revealing of the mirrors into which we look.

## Action into Language

That this obvious fact was obvious to Hemingway is a matter of record. Long before he had money enough for a safari or time enough to compose a theory of esthetics, had he ever wished to compose one, he had learned that lesson. Of the time in his 20's when he was learning to write, he said, "I found the greatest difficulty, aside from knowing truly what you really felt, rather than what you were supposed to feel . . . was to put down what really happened in action; what the actual things were which produced the emotion that you experienced." The problem, that is to say, was to master the collision of man and event writer and experience in *both* its terms: the perception of the event as it really was and the recognition of the emotion that the event really excited. A later remark of his added another dimension to the task. In a letter to a young man who had sent him some imitative work he said, ". . . see the things you write about not through my eyes and my ears but through your own with your language." To see "with language," to see "what really happened in action" and to recognize "what you really felt rather than what you were supposed to feel," *with language* was a writer's task as Hemingway saw it. Most writers I think would agree that the task was well seen and that accomplishment of the task so defined would be anything but a betrayal of the obligation which every writer assumes. To put together what "really" happened and what you "really" felt as you faced it is not only to see the lion but to understand the man. The writer who can do this, as Hemingway demonstrated that he could, is no less a poet of the human experience—God's spy—than the writer who spies upon nearer and more familiar worlds.

What became of Hemingway? Fame became of him, yes, but something more, I think, than fame. Art became of him—became of him in the truest and the largest sense. [German poet Rainer M.] Rilke once said of the writing of a verse: it is not enough merely to feel; one must also see and touch and know. But it is not enough either, to see and touch and know: one must have memories of love and pain and death. But not even these memories are enough: the memories must be "turned to blood within us" so that they are no longer distinguishable from ourselves. Experience, Rilke was declaring, must turn into man before a poem can be written. Experience, that is to say, must reach such an intensity that it contains our own being. When that happens—when experience and man *so* meet—the poem may be written and when the poem is written we may discover who we are. Hemingway brought himself to face experience of this intensity not once, but more than once. And what became of him was that great triumph.

# The Berlin Crisis and the Rise of the Berlin Wall

## By the U.S. Department of State

On August 13, 1961, the Soviet Union sealed the border crossing between East and West Berlin with barbed-wire barriers and began construction on the Berlin Wall, the visible Cold War scar dividing the Communist East from the democratic West. This act of aggression violated the 1945 Potsdam Agreement signed by the United States, Britain, and the Soviet Union at the end of World War II. The parties had agreed that a divided, postwar Germany was to be treated as a single economic unit and eventually reestablished as one nation.

The following excerpt was taken from a pamphlet on the Berlin crisis produced by the U.S. Department of State for the general public in late August 1961. It describes the division of Berlin after World War II, the Soviet Union's plans for absorbing West Berlin into Soviet-ruled East Germany, and the rise of the Berlin Wall. The pamphlet illustrates how the impasse over Berlin brought the two superpowers to the brink of war, prompting President Kennedy to announce to the American people on July 25, 1961, that he had ordered U.S. troops to prepare for combat and that nuclear war was a very real possibility. The Berlin crisis receded in the fall of 1962 after the Soviet installment of missiles in Cuba presented a more pressing threat to the United States.

U.S. Department of State, "Background: Berlin—1961," *U.S. Department of State Publication 7257*, August 1961, pp. 1–2, 15, 17–18, 20–23, 26–29.

**B**erlin lies more than 100 miles behind the Iron Curtain within the Soviet-occupied zone of Germany. It is not, however, part of that zone. It is a separate political entity for which the four major allies of the war against Nazi tyranny are jointly responsible. Its special status stems from the fact that it was the capital not only of Hitler's Third Reich but of the German nation formed in the latter half of the 19th century. In essence, the four major allies agreed to hold Berlin, as the traditional capital, in trust for a democratic and united Germany.

The Federal Republic of Germany, comprising the former occupation zones of the Western Allies, is a democratic state. Its 53 million people enjoy self-determination at all levels. Through their freely elected Federal Government, they have taken their place in the community of free nations.

By contrast, the 16 million inhabitants of the eastern zone are ruled by the Soviet Union through its Communist creature, the East German regime which calls itself the "German Democratic Republic." *That regime is neither democratic nor a republic.* It was not chosen by the people it controls and has never been freely endorsed by them. It was imposed by duress and is maintained by all the oppressive apparatus of a police state backed by the military forces of the Soviet Union.

Berlin contains four sectors. The 2,250,000 inhabitants of its three western sectors live under a municipal government which they have freely chosen. The eastern sector has some 1,100,000 inhabitants. In 1948, in violation of their commitments, the Soviets separated it from the rest of the city. Subsequently, in further violation of their commitments, they permitted their German agents to declare it the capital of the East German regime. Thus the people of East Berlin, like those of the eastern zone of Germany, are ruled by a regime they did not choose.

*The government of West Berlin is the only freely elected government behind either the Iron or the Bamboo Curtains.* Repeatedly the Soviets and their German agents have sought to blot out this island of freedom. Their methods have ranged from the brazen to the devious, but their purpose has always been clear.

Every President of the United States since the Second World War has deemed the defense of Free Berlin critical to the security of the United States and of the entire free world. The United Kingdom, France, and the United States stand pledged to defend West Berlin by whatever means may be necessary. All the members of the North Atlantic Treaty Organization [NATO] stand pledged to support them in discharging that obligation. These solemn commitments were not undertaken lightly. . . .

In the last 16 years an estimated 3,300,000 Germans have fled East Germany and East Berlin. More than 2,600,000 of these have left since records began to be kept in West Berlin and the Federal German Republic in 1949. Since 1953 the border between East Germany and the Federal Republic has been dangerous for a refugee to try to cross. The Communists guard it with barbed wire, watchtowers with sharpshooters, and a "death strip" of plowed earth. However, until August 1961 a refugee who reached East Berlin could cross to West Berlin on foot or by subway or the elevated line—provided he acted like a commuter and carried no telltale luggage. Consequently, a large majority of the refugees from East Germany have escaped via West Berlin, whence most have been transported by air to refugee camps in the German Federal Republic. In these centers arrangements are made for their housing and employment in West Germany.

Over the years, the German Communists applied increasingly strict measures to curb this trek to freedom. A refugee caught in the act was made liable to imprisonment. So were his close relatives if they remained behind. Contrary to Communist propaganda, the German Federal Republic, the government of Free Berlin, and the Western Powers did not encourage the exodus. In fact, high officials of the Federal Republic often appealed to the population of the Soviet zone to remain there as long as possible. They do not want to see East Germany depleted of its most stalwart elements. Above all, they do not want to give the Soviets an excuse to move non-German workers into East Germany. (Communist rule combined with the West Berlin "escape hatch" to give East Germany a unique distinction in the world of today: a shrinking population.)

Nevertheless, the flow of refugees continued. The rate varied but in recent years averaged about 4,000 a week. The refugees have included a high percentage of East German physicians and men and women of various other professions but *most have been workers fleeing "the paradise of the workers."* Significantly also, a majority have been young people—approximately 50 percent under 25 years of age. They were 9 years or younger when the Soviets and their German puppets began to try to make them into Communists. (Incidentally, the German lass who won the Miss

Universe contest at Miami in July 1961, had fled East Germany only a year earlier. She is an electronics engineer.)

The continuing westward trek of East Germans and East Berliners who decided to "vote with their feet" was an eloquent judgment on Communist rule. . . .

Through wise policies, driving initiative, and hard work, West Germany's economic recovery surged forward. Its rate of increase in gross national product became one of the highest in the world.

For 12 years now West Germany has been a fully functioning political democracy, with regular free elections at all levels from local to national, free speech, and all the other rights and safeguards for individual liberty essential to a self-governing society.

In these same 12 years, East Germany has moved just as rapidly in the opposite direction: toward increasing regimentation, collectivization, and progressive strangulation of individual liberties.

As West Berlin remains under joint Allied trusteeship, it is not part of the German Federal Republic. But naturally the association between these two self-governing areas is close. The Federal Republic contributes to the economy and cultural life of Free Berlin. Free Berlin has representatives in the Federal Parliament in Bonn, although they do not vote.

## The Quest for a German Peace Settlement

After Joseph Stalin's death and the Korean truce in 1953, the Western Allies resumed their efforts to obtain a peace settlement for Germany as a whole. Another meeting of the foreign ministers, convened in Berlin January 25, 1954, proved fruitless. The Soviets made plain their resolve to keep East Germany in captivity and to permit its unification with West Germany only under conditions which would favor the extension of Communist control over all of Germany.

The Austrian peace treaty, formally known as the Austrian State Treaty, to which the Soviets finally acceded in May 1955, rekindled hope. And at the summit conference in Geneva in July 1955, the Heads of Government of the Big Four agreed, in a directive to their foreign ministers, that "the settlement of the German question and the reunification of Germany by means of free elections shall be carried out in conformity with the national interests of the German people and the interests of European security."

At the subsequent foreign ministers meeting, convened in October 1955, the Western Powers submitted proposals in full harmony with that directive. The Soviets insisted that unification be effected only by agreement between "two German states." The fruitless conference adjourned on November 16. . . .

In July 1957 the Western Powers, including the Federal Republic, tried again to reopen negotiations, coupling the reunification of Germany with European security arrangements which offered far-reaching assurances to the Soviet Union. Again they found themselves up against a stone wall.

In December 1957 the Soviet Union called for a new summit conference. After consultation with NATO members President Dwight Eisenhower agreed to participate, provided that the groundwork was laid through diplomatic channels and the foreign ministers. But the exchanges which followed yielded no progress.

## The Second Major Assault on Free Berlin

Late in 1958 the Soviet Union launched its second major assault on the freedom of West Berlin. The attack began with a speech by Nikita Khrushchev on November 10, another on November 26, and a note to the Western Powers on November 27, 1958. In that note the Soviet Union said that it considered null and void all of its agreements with the Western Allies as to Berlin and demanded the withdrawal of Western military forces from the city. It proposed to make West Berlin a demilitarized "free city." As to the reunification of Germany, it proposed that "the two German states" enter into negotiations looking toward a confederation (without free elections in the eastern zone).

The Soviet note set a deadline of 6 months. It said that if the Western Allies had not acceded to its demands by then, the Soviet Union would sign a peace treaty with the "German Democratic Republic" and turn over to it control of all access routes to Berlin.

The Soviet note, like so many other documents emanating from Moscow, was replete with omissions and distortions.

A few fundamental points may be noted here: *The Soviet Union cannot take away the rights and obligations of the Western Powers to remain in and protect Free Berlin*. Those rights and obligations were not conferred by the Soviet Union but are rooted in the Nazi surrender. They include the right of access to Berlin. Likewise, the Soviet Union cannot unilaterally annul or modify its agreements with the Western Allies as to Berlin, including its guarantees of access to the city. Those agreements can be altered only by consent of all Four Powers.

In its reply of December 31, 1958, the United States rejected the Soviet demands and said that it could not embark on discussions with the Soviet Union "under menace or ultimatum." It nevertheless inquired if the Soviet Union were ready to enter into discussions among the Four Powers on the question of Berlin "in the wider framework of negotiations for a solution of the German problem as well as that of European security." Similar replies were sent by the United Kingdom and France.

On January 10, 1959, the Soviet Union proposed the calling of a peace conference and summit talks on Berlin and Germany, with participation by the "German Democratic Republic" and the Federal Republic of Germany. It did not mention, although it did not withdraw, the 6-month deadline.

Construing this as an implicit retreat from duress, the Western Powers on February 16 informed the Soviet Government that they were prepared to take part in a Four Power Conference of Foreign Ministers to deal with the problem of Germany in all its aspects. They consented that German "advisers" be invited.

The Soviets eventually agreed. The Foreign Ministers Conference opened in Geneva on May 11, 1959. Representatives of the Federal Republic and of the East German regime were permitted to be present as advisers.

## The Western Peace Plan vs. the Soviet Plan

On May 14, 1959, the Western Allies put forward a comprehensive peace plan which reached far to accommodate Soviet interests and views. It was a phased plan which did not insist on immediate free elections in East Germany but provided time for a mixed German committee to draft an electoral law and work out plans for increased trade and other contacts between the two parts of Germany. Interlocked with a series of steps toward the reunification of Germany were provisions for measures against surprise attack and for progressive reductions in military forces both in an area of Europe and by overall ceilings on Soviet and U.S. military personnel.

*This far-reaching plan, to be applied by stages, was designed to consolidate peace in Europe, east and west. The Soviets rejected it out of hand.*

The Soviet plan, presented on May 15, called for:

1. Separate peace treaties with the "two German states," the negotiation of reunification to be left to them, with no time limit,

thus no assurance that Germany would ever be reunited or that free elections would ever be permitted in East Germany.

2. Pending German reunification, West Berlin to become a "free, demilitarized city," thus "occupation" by the Western Powers to end.

3. The NATO powers to withdraw their forces and dismantle all military bases on "foreign territory." The Soviets, in return, to withdraw their forces from East Germany, Poland, and Hungary.

The first point, when combined with the third, became a plan to weaken the security of West Germany, and indeed of all Free Europe, thus opening the way for eventual extension of the Communist domain. . . .

## The Plan for a "Demilitarized Free City"

The term "demilitarized free city" is appealing. As West Berlin is already a free city, the key word is "demilitarized."

No one could seriously argue that the small contingents of Western troops in West Berlin, which in July 1961 numbered only 11,000, are a threat to peace. They are surrounded by 22 or more Soviet divisions plus the armed forces of the East German regime. In 16 years they have not been responsible for a single provocative incident. They are kept there as proof and warning that the Western Allies will protect the freedom of West Berlin, come what may. . . .

If the Soviets really want to see the freedom of West Berlin preserved, why do they insist on a change in the present arrangement, which guarantees that freedom while preserving the peace? Khrushchev says that, since many years have elapsed since the Nazi surrender, it is time to do away with the occupation agreements. Those agreements could have been dispensed with years ago if the Soviets had complied with them. If they had done so, or would do so now, there would be no Berlin problem and no German problem. But they still prevent by force both the unification of Germany, which would automatically settle the Berlin question, and a free expression of will by the people of East Germany and East Berlin on that or anything else. . . .

In gauging Khrushchev's real intentions regarding West Berlin, one should observe that the Soviet note of November 27, 1958, stated that "the most correct and natural" solution would be to absorb West Berlin into the "German Democratic Republic." Soviet Foreign Minister Andrei Gromyko reiterated on May 30:

If we are to speak frankly, the Soviet Government considers the creation of a Free City far from being an ideal solution of the West Berlin question. The most equitable approach to this question would be, of course, the extension to West Berlin of the full sovereignty of the German Democratic Republic. I think that the German Democratic Republic, whose capital the division of the city continues to mutilate, could with the fullest justification demand such a solution of the question.

The Soviet plan to make West Berlin a "demilitarized free city" is thus obviously intended as a temporary way station on the road to "the most correct and natural" solution. . . .

## Khrushchev's War Threat

Since November 1958, Khrushchev has repeatedly warned that if the Western Allies did not settle the Berlin and German questions on terms satisfactory to him he would sign a separate peace treaty with the East German regime and turn over to it control of the access routes to Berlin.

Nobody can prevent Moscow from signing a "peace treaty" with this or any other of its puppets. Such an act would be simply a ventriloquist stunt.

The threat to peace begins with the Communist contention, contrary to international law, that such a "peace treaty" would annul Western rights pertaining to Berlin. The threat to destroy those rights implies action to prevent their exercise. The Western Allies can accept neither the legality nor the potential practical consequences of that position. For example, as free access is indispensable to the survival in freedom of West Berlin, it is the inescapable duty of the Western Allies to see that free access is not blocked, interrupted, or whittled away. Yet the East German regime, which according to Khrushchev would control all access routes on conclusion of a "peace treaty," is a member of the Warsaw military pact, of which the Soviet Union is the architect and chief member. *This, in essence, is what makes Khrushchev's declared intention a grave threat to peace.* . . .

## The Third Assault and the Rise of the Berlin Wall

Khrushchev did not wait long, however. He indicated during the winter and early spring months that he still regarded Berlin and

Germany as urgent questions. Meanwhile he was promoting or aggravating trouble in Laos and elsewhere and making bellicose speeches.

President Kennedy decided, and Khrushchev concurred, that a direct exchange of views, without attempting negotiations, might be useful. These talks were held June 3–4, 1961, in Vienna. They were, in President Kennedy's word, "somber."

A Soviet aide memoire on Germany and Berlin, delivered June 4, marked the formal beginning of the third great assault on the freedom of Berlin. The Western Allies replied on July 17. The text of the U.S. reply is self-explanatory.

The circumstances and tone of the third assault, together with Khrushchev's belligerent words at Vienna and elsewhere, suggest that in manufacturing another crisis over West Berlin the Soviets have far-reaching aims.

The third assault on the freedom of West Berlin produced reactions which Khrushchev perhaps did not anticipate. President Kennedy recommended and the U.S. Congress promptly authorized a substantial expansion and strengthening of the American armed forces. Corresponding steps were taken by other NATO members. Among these and other reactions, not least significant was a sudden rise in the outflow of East Germans and East Berliners. In July 1961 more than 30,000 found refuge in the West—nearly twice the previous monthly average.

The East German authorities instituted new measures to stem the flow. They restricted travel from East Germany to East Berlin. In Berlin, through more frequent checks and interrogations, they stopped and turned back some of the refugees trying to escape across the sector border. They look steps to force some 50,000 East Berliners working in West Berlin to give up their jobs. They supported these and related steps with an intensive propaganda campaign, which ranged from branding refugees as "traitors" to inventing a "polio epidemic" in West Germany.

Day after day the efforts of the East German authorities became more frantic. They probably succeeded in blocking the flight of many thousands who were seeking freedom. But they did not stop the exodus. More than 22,000 refugees arrived in West Berlin in the first 12 days of August.

On August 13, 1961, the Communists took the desperate step of sealing the Berlin sector border against East Germans and East Berliners. Shortly after midnight a communique was published by the Warsaw Pact nations (the Soviet Union and its European satellites), calling for such action. It was accompanied by a decree of the "German Democratic Republic" prohibiting East Germans and East Berliners from entering West Berlin. East German troops and armed police, with armored cars and tanks, were deployed along the entire sector border. They put up barbed wire barriers. (A few days later they began building a wall of cement blocks.) Other East German troops were deployed on the edges of the city. These in turn were backed by a ring of troops from three Soviet divisions, including one tank division. These large-scale supporting deployments were obviously intended to inhibit a popular arising such as had occurred in East Berlin and East Germany in 1953 and in Hungary in 1956.

Thus was the escape hatch from the East German prison slammed shut and locked. And thus once again was it demonstrated that the Communists can maintain their rule only by force.

The closing of the sector border and the deployment of East German troops in East Berlin were further violations of Soviet pledges. The Western Allies protested, but with no immediate result.

## The Allied Trusteeship: What the Record Shows

The record shows that the Western Allies have been faithful to the trusteeship they assumed in 1945. They have fostered the reconstruction of Germany as a peaceable, self-governing nation. They have fostered and protected free institutions in West Berlin.

The record shows that the Soviet Union, which joined in the same pledges, has dishonored them by a long series of nonfeasances, misfeasances, and malfeasances. It shows that the Soviet Union has violated, flagrantly and repeatedly, its wartime and postwar agreements on the occupation and rehabilitation of Germany and on the special status of Berlin.

The Soviet Union has prevented the reunification of Germany. It has denied democratic self-government and self-determination to the people of East Germany and East Berlin, instead imposing on them and maintaining by force a police-state regime. It armed that regime. In these and many other ways it broke its agreements.

The Soviet Union separated East Berlin from the rest of the city. It permitted its East German puppet to proclaim Berlin as its capital. It permitted its East German puppet to parade, and finally to station, troops and tanks in East Berlin. It has now sealed the sector border against East Germans and East Berliners wishing to go to West Berlin. In these and many other ways it has broken its clear-cut agreements with its wartime allies as to the special status of Greater Berlin.

Not content with inflicting its will on the peoples of East Germany and East Berlin, the Soviet Union has repeatedly tried to force or suffocate the people of West Berlin into submission to Communist tyranny.

No one who believes in self-determination could be deaf to the clearly expressed wish of the people of Free Berlin. They have made it unmistakably clear that they want the Western Allies to stay as guardians and are adamantly opposed to any weakening in the protection they now enjoy.

The status of Berlin was a key issue in the West Berlin elections of December 1958, held just after Khrushchev issued his ultimatum. The candidates of the SED (Communist Party) advocated a change. All other candidates of all other parties opposed any change. The Communists were as free as the others to advocate their cause. (Indeed, West Berlin police and firemen broke up anti-Communist demonstrations against Communist political rallies.) Ninety-six percent of the electorate voted. The Communists received only 1.9 percent of the vote cast. Such was the verdict of a people who know what communism means because they are surrounded by it.

## The Free World's Stake in Berlin

West Berlin is a lighthouse of freedom in a dark totalitarian sea. It demonstrates the material superiorities of a free society which allows and encourages individual initiative. More important, it is a shining model of political, intellectual, and spiritual freedom in which individual liberties are assured and the people choose those who govern them.

Khrushchev and his followers profess to want "peaceful co-existence" and "peaceful competition." For more than a decade Berlin has been a test tube of peaceful competition. Hundreds of thousands of visitors have seen at first hand the result—that the difference between West and East Berlin is the difference between day and night.

For the peoples of East Berlin and East Germany, the special status of Berlin holds the hope of their eventual reunion with the people of the Federal Republic in a united democratic German nation. For many of them, until mid-August 1961, West Berlin was a venthole in the prison wall—a place they could visit now and then for a life-sustaining breath of free air. For those of them who could no longer endure Communist tyranny it was, until then, the escape hatch to freedom.

For all the peoples held in captivity in the vast detention camp which is Eastern Europe, West Berlin is a beacon of hope—a hope nourished since 1948 by the ability of the Western Powers and the Berliners to maintain its freedom.

Of all this, Khrushchev and his German Communist puppets are painfully aware. That is why West Berlin is to Khrushchev a "cancerous tumor" and a "bone stuck in our throat." That is why he has publicly declared his resolve "to eradicate this splinter from the heart of Europe."

For the Western Allies, Free Berlin is the symbol, the evidence, and the acid test of their unity, strength, and determination. It has become in a real sense the keystone of the defensive arch of NATO. Were the Western Allies to permit the freedom of West Berlin to be lost, whether by direct assault or by erosion, they would be false to their pledges. Who would trust their word again? And if they, who are the backbone of the security of the free world, should falter and fall apart, what hope would remain for freedom anywhere?

Berlin is a focal point in a worldwide struggle. The central issue in that struggle is, in the words of Secretary of State Dean Rusk: ". . . the announced determination to impose a world of coercion upon those not already subjected to it. . . . At stake is the survival and growth of the world of free choice and . . . free cooperation." That central issue, he pointed out, "is posed between the Sino-Soviet empire and all the rest, whether allied or neutral; and it is now posed in every continent."

All peoples throughout the globe who enjoy or aspire to freedom, including the captive peoples of the Communist empires, have a vital interest in the preservation of freedom—of self-determination—in West Berlin. In defending Free Berlin we defend not only Bonn, Paris, London, Oslo, Ottawa, Washington, Kansas City, Boise, but, in fact, every citizen in the North Atlantic community. Equally we defend New Delhi, Kuala Lumpur, Tokyo, Lagos, Tunis, Cairo, Rio de Janeiro, Montevideo, and every other city and village and people who wish to be free.

Everyone who treasures freedom can join the stouthearted Free Berliners in saying to Khrushchev and his Communist satraps what two emissaries of a free city of ancient Greece said to a Persian satrap who asked them why they did not submit to the Persian tyrant Xerxes. They replied, according to Herodotus: "You have experience of half the matter; but the other half is beyond your knowledge. The life of a slave you understand; but, never having tasted liberty, you can never know whether it be sweet or not. But ah! had you known what freedom is, you would bid us fight for it, not with the spear only, but with the battle-axe."

# Nuclear War and the Debate over Family Fallout Shelters

## By Margaret Mead

In the summer of 1961, worsening U.S. relations with the Soviet Union incited President John F. Kennedy to announce that "prudent" families should construct fallout shelters as protection against a nuclear attack. Publications like *Life* magazine and *Popular Mechanics* offered tips and plans to frightened Americans for building backyard shelters. These were to be dug underground and stocked with water, canned goods, and other essentials.

In the following essay, Margaret Mead questions the president's inclusion of shelters in his civil defense program. She argues that reliance on individual shelters would lead to glaring inequalities, leaving poor urban dwellers without the means to construct shelters defenseless. According to Mead, Americans can prevent nuclear war by demonstrating to the rest of the world that they support peace and an end to the arms race with the Soviet Union. The author was a highly regarded anthropologist known for her studies of primitive societies. She died in 1978.

In the cold war of nerves, the state of morale in the opposing countries is an essential ingredient of defense, part of the huge paraphernalia of deterrence each side has assembled.

Margaret Mead, "Are Shelters the Answer?" *New York Times Magazine*, September 26, 1961, pp. 29, 124–26.

But given the differences between the American and the Soviet systems, each country necessarily goes about building civilian morale differently. In contrast to the Soviet Union, we have announced publicly that civilian defense is part of our program of deterrence.

## Questioning Bomb Shelters

From one point of view, the assurance that Americans have the will and the intention to survive any kind of attack should introduce one more beneficent pause into the Soviet Union's calculations. There are, however, some questions. Can the civilian defense program we are now developing really produce the steadfastness, the resolute determination neither to surrender nor to allow ourselves to be panicked into provocation or attack? Does it convey to those who might attack us that we are—or are not—expecting to be attacked? Is the program, in fact, a deterrent or a provocation?

This past summer Western Europe resonated with horror to reports that some Americans were planning to build individual bomb shelters in which each man would defend his own family, by force of arms if necessary, against his less provident neighbors. Many Europeans who had survived the agonies of warfare against civilians, sharing space and air with all who needed shelter, took these stories as one more example of Americans' inexplicable affinity for violence. In their eyes, Americans had accepted the idea of war—a war that would destroy the rest of mankind—for the sake of a set of principles that, if these stories were to be believed, would not stand up to a single bombing.

Set beside such terms as "overkill" and "megadeath," the picture of members of the richest and most technically advanced country in the world regressing to a level lower than that of any savages, to the level of trapped animals, made Europeans shudder. Perhaps the world did not have to wait for a nuclear war to bring about the physical dissolution of civilization: perhaps it was dissolving morally now.

New stories added new details to the picture. A clergyman sanctioned the right of a man to kill his neighbor in order to protect his own family—a right accorded to no member of a society which calls itself a society. A nation-wide television program, depicting the fictional response to an alert, showed a frantic group of neighbors battering down in violent rage a family's shelter which, once destroyed, could protect no one.

What such stories suggested was that the Government, by giving its blessing to the construction of individual shelters, had abnegated its historic responsibility to defend the people of the United States and severed the ties that should bind together any men and their government in an emergency. Instead of fostering the shared responsibility that makes all men equal because all share the danger, the admonition to build individual shelters would make rich and poor, city dweller and suburban dweller, householder and tenant, glaringly unequal.

It is, of course, easy for the critical student of civilian morale and of American culture to point out that in a real emergency Americans never have behaved in this way and never would do so. It is easy to recall [novelist] Neville Shute's misanthropic prophecy, before World War II, that the threat of bombing would send the English rushing off to save their individual families, with catastrophic results for everyone. History has recorded that the English did no such thing. And the research undertaken immediately after World War II to study American behavior in major disaster situations is equally an attestation not to men caught in a flood who push clinging hands off precariously overloaded logs, but to men who jeopardize their own lives to rescue those in danger.

## Temporary Hysteria

Even Mr. Shute, disillusioned in old age with his new country, Australia, and writing [the nuclear war novel] On the Beach to convict Australians of apathy, pictured Australian men and women as kind and protective of one another in the months before they succumbed to the certain death which they had been too politically uninterested to prevent. But when the movie version of On the Beach opened simultaneously in some dozen major cities around the world, including Moscow, the official Soviet comment scored the passivity of a people who did not struggle to the very end to find a solution that would ensure the continuity of human life.

Looking critically at our own responses to the shelter issue, we could comfortably decide that they reflect no more than a temporary hysteria which need not be taken seriously. On the general theory that neither our allies nor our enemies ever understand us, we could shrug off the fact that our current plans and our present behavior dismay our Western European allies and seem to confirm the Soviet view of our disunity and lack of responsibility for one another. We could settle back and say: Given time American generosity and good sense will reassert itself.

In fact, people have come to realize that there would be only a one-in-three chance of a family's being together when an attack came, that community shelters would give far more assurance to men separated from their families by the length of a city, and to mothers whose children were blocks away in school, than could any individual shelter, however well-stocked with food and medical supplies and adorned with a fake picture window. So also, people are coming to recognize that only by helping one another would there be any hope of survival.

If money and effort are still to go into building shelters, the Government, in time, will assume its responsibilities to help actively, and members of city blocks and suburban tracts will work together to build places where, in an emergency, cooperative friendliness would increase in direct proportion to the hazards the group encountered. With the restoration of this much good sense, individual towns will stop their plans to construct barriers and will make preparations to receive and keep those who, in a real bombing, would be fleeing from disaster.

This is not enough, however. It does not meet one very present difficulty.

*President Kennedy urged Americans to construct fallout shelters to protect themselves in the event of a nuclear attack.*

The United States shelter program, we are told, is designed not for real action but as deterrence, to meet a situation we are determined shall never occur. It is designed for its psychological and moral effect on Soviet leadership.

Those of us who realize that Soviet young people have been brought up convinced that their Government seeks peace, that it has been forced into warlike preparations only by the "hostile and aggressive acts" of the "imperialistic capitalists," are aware of the total commitment with which these young people would exert any effort their leaders required of them. The thought has a sobering effect upon us. In like manner, we hope that our stance of steadfastness, our high purpose and clear morale will have a sobering effect on Soviet leaders.

## A New Understanding of Warfare

But can the picture we have given the world have such a sobering effect? Could any picture of the whole nation planning to dig itself in, whether family by family or community by community, regardless of the fate of the rest of the world, have such a sobering effect? The answer, obviously, is: No.

Before we go further, then, it may be worth-while for us to examine what has happened—what our behavior is symptomatic of—and to take thought what we can do.

I believe that the fantastic, unrealistic, morally dangerous behavior in which citizenry and government have indulged in thinking about the shelter program was an expression of a much wider ethical conflict—one in which Americans have been involved ever since we dropped the first nuclear bomb on Hiroshima, and which has affected all our subsequent views of world problems.

One effect of this event was to turn Americans outward to the rest of the world. An era had ended that had lasted from the time warfare was invented, and it was clear suddenly that no principle, no cause, no group, no loved land could in the future be successfully defended by warfare. In a war, all combatants would be risking—if not actually committing —suicide and the destruction of their own civilization.

In the process, they also would be committing murder against all bystanders. In the past, no matter what kingdoms fell or what civilizations crumbled, the march of mankind could continue. But this is no longer true.

With this recognition came the realization that we were no

longer protected by fixed boundaries. This recognition, this new awareness, activated many kinds of expansion. We extended our defenses around the world. We visualized new frontiers in outer space and in the depths of the oceans. We expanded our support of trans-national activities of all sorts, through the United Nations and bilaterally, through the kind of programs that led to the I.G.Y.[1] through aid programs and the Peace Corps.

## Retreat from Others

With a tremendous lift and pull of our national muscles, we were reaching out into membership in the human race, in a planetary community that existed *de facto* though not yet in theory.

Countering this centrifugal movement was the centripetal pull of fear and dread—dread of the danger of mass destruction with which mankind now must live, perhaps forever; dread of the strain of living always related to distant and still alien peoples and having somehow to assimilate their experiences, good and bad, to our own; dread of the vast population spurt that is already being likened to an atomic explosion; and, closer to home, dread of the surging masses of young people, uneducated and unprepared for urban living, turning to drugs and crime; dread of our crumbling, dangerous cities.

As American feeling was stretched to the utmost, moving even further outward, those who were ill-prepared to take these unexpected, giant steps turned inward. Drawn back in space and in time, hiding from the future and the rest of the world, they turned to the green suburb, protected by zoning laws against members of other classes or races or religions, and concentrated on the single, tight little family.

They idealized the life of each such family living alone in self-sufficient togetherness, protecting its members against the contamination of different ways or others' needs. Several years ago, two sociologists, one of them a clergyman, advised Americans that the way to preserve their families was to eschew all contact with any family that had any problem of delinquency or mental health, even a family broken by death. The armed, individual shelter is the logical end of this retreat from trust in and responsibility for others.

---

1. The International Geophysical Year (1957–1958) project allowed scientists from around the world to take part in coordinated experiments concerning geophysical phenomena.

## The Necessity of Peace

Yet even though we recognize the present shelter program and the American people's response to it to be symptomatic, we need not regard the current discussion as a total waste. The debate about shelters has caused an upsurge of genuine, realistic concern about nuclear war. Americans can refocus this concern into a greater understanding and acceptance of the responsibility carried by the nation which first invented the bomb and, so far, is the only one to have used it. In turn, this can become a mandate for a national effort to invent ways to protect the peoples of the world from a war which might end in the extinction of the human species.

The first step in the direction of a world rule of law is the recognition that peace no longer is an unobtainable ideal but a necessary condition of continued human existence. But to take even this step we must return to a calm and responsible frame of mind, a frame of mind in which we can face the long patient tasks ahead. This means finding a workable resolution of the present confused, panicky, incoherent discussion of the shelter problem itself.

To do this, what do we need? Most immediately, we need clarification of the facts. We need a clear, frank statement of the differences among blast effects, avoidable fallout effects, and long-term death and mutation. We need as clear a formulation as possible of what the risks of an all-out nuclear war would be for ourselves and for every other people on earth, what the chances would be that, given the survival of some human beings, it would be possible to reorganize something resembling the free society we wish to protect.

This knowledge would help the American people to judge what it is we are trying to prevent by deterrence, how essential it is to find some safer solution. Judgment that is based on knowledge should strengthen our determination both to support our present policy of deterrence and to work unsparingly to end the spiraling arms race.

But the damage to our trust in our Government, our physical scientists and ourselves cannot be undone simply by refocusing our concern onto the safety of the human race. Those who cannot protect their own people cannot undertake to protect others.

## Disaster Programs

First, we must knit together the fragments of our trust in our national leadership, our communities and our neighborhoods. This requires some conspicuous national action protective of our people. The discussion of the dangers that would follow a nuclear attack has opened up many other fears—fears of the effects of fire, of tornados and earthquakes, of armed bandits roving through the land, of the breakdown of neighborliness, of the unwillingness of intact communities to help those who flee from disaster. These fears must be allayed.

One way of doing this would be to undertake, now, a nationally underwritten program which would initiate in each town and city, each rural region of the country, a Protective Disaster Program, adequate to meet the different kinds of disaster, natural and man-made, to which we are all too often subject. Centers, each fitted out with food, water, medical supplies and communications devices, and with a core group of people familiar with an area, a center and each other, could be a permanent source of protection.

Our present handling of disasters is, for the most part, on an *ad hoc* basis, with help rushed to the scene after the fire is raging. We have not had—and we should now build—a national system of community protection with continuing use of our vast resources of professional and volunteer personnel. Multipurpose centers of this kind, within a national framework, would meet any demand for protection against fallout—in the remote eventuality that protection was needed.

## Inclusive Nationhood

Beyond this, however, is the problem of escape from the double pull of expansion and contraction in which we have become entrapped and which has been expressed by the arguments over shelters. For this we need a new formulation of the tasks confronting us.

The nation-state, advanced by warfare and given time to consolidate peaceful internal gains by periods of truce, was a great social invention on mankind's long road toward higher levels of political integration. Now we need a further social invention that will give us a way of extending our responsibility, based on our own nationhood, beyond our borders. We need a way of including not only our allies and the uncommitted nations but even our enemies, *while they are our enemies.*

No more than the father of a family guarding an individual shelter, or the little town arming itself against refugees from the city, can a single nation protect its people unless it also protects the rest of mankind, with or without their consent. This is a form of nationhood that is just on the edge of being invented.

Our sense of overexpansion, our sense of unbearable responsibility for so much and so many, can be eased as we do this by the realization that one of the conditions of life in the modern world is that matched adversaries like the United States and the Soviet Union try to outdo each other in every respect. Refusal on our part to face the real issues can only lead to a spread of irresponsibility in the Soviet Union. As we assume responsibility for preventing the Soviet Union from committing suicide, taking us and the rest of the world down with it, the Soviets, too, may be expected to assume reciprocal responsibilities. At present they have been attempting to outdo us in explosive deterrence. There is no reason why they should not equally attempt to outdo us in stated responsibility.

The more expansive we become in our willingness to take responsibility not only for our children but for all children, including the children of our enemies, the more we can mobilize our energies and the energies of the world to bring into being these new forms of nationhood.

# ARTICLE 11

# Freedom-Fighting Guitars: The Popularity of Folk Music

**By Nat Hentoff**

Folk music grew increasingly popular throughout 1961, coinciding with a rising interest in social justice and political activism on college campuses across the country. Historically music of the poor and oppressed, college-educated young people updated early–twentieth century folk songs with socially conscious lyrics. Performers would typically sing against racism, war, and the government while accompanying themselves on acoustic guitars.

In the following assessment of the folk music trend, critic Nat Hentoff describes many of the "citybillies" he has heard on records and in coffeehouses as shrill amateurs with a tendency toward militant self-righteousness. Nevertheless, Hentoff finds a legitimate artistry in the music of Joan Baez, who would go on to perform with 1960s icon Bob Dylan, and a New York City group calling themselves the New Lost City Ramblers. Hentoff writes a weekly music column for the *Village Voice* and remains a preeminent music critic.

Nat Hentoff, "The Rise of Folkum Music," *Commonweal*, vol. 75, October 20, 1961, pp. 99–100.

In a Greenwich Village [neighborhood in New York City] refuge for apprentice sophisticates a few weeks ago, a smooth young man announced from the bandstand that he would let us in on a vintage Southern mountain ballad. "I don't know exactly where it came from," he said with what I presume was guilelessness. "In fact, I don't know much of anything about it. But I sure do like it." Predictably, the performance was as blandly amateurish as the Sunday afternoon come-all-ye's at Washington Square [park in Greenwich Village], where civil liberties triumphed over aesthetics earlier this year [folk singers were temporarily banned from the park]. ("Mayor Wagner," comedian Lenny Bruce observed at the time, "was simply expressing a musical fact. He didn't mean, 'They *can't* sing.' He was just pointing out they can't *sing.*")

## More Folkum than Folk

Certainly not all the eager citybillies who are finding twangy status in rummaging through the [Francis J.] Child [nineteenth-century composer of the *English and Scottish Popular Ballads*, considered the "canon" of folk music] ballads and other pre-Mitch Miller [1940s music producer] songs are ignorant of the music's context. Many of them have swallowed large parts of the Lomax books of collected folk tunes,[1] and there are even a few who own some of the Library of Congress discs that were recorded in the field by farmers, lumberjacks, and housewives who weren't aware they were artists until the man with the portable recording machine assured them they were.

Those of the citybillies, moreover, who go on to make itinerant careers of their enthusiasm generally find it necessary to do some sporadic research, if only to defend themselves against querulous purists in their audiences. Nonetheless, an increasingly high percentage of what is being presented as folk music in night clubs, coffee houses and on records is much more folkum than folk. (So far as I can determine, the term "folkum" was first insistently used by the scathingly honest monthly *Little Sandy Review*—the apoplectic conscience of the folk industry.)

It is easy enough to skewer the obvious medicine men—Harry Belafonte, the Kingston Trio, the Brothers Four, the self-parodying

---

1. John Lomax and his son Alan traveled the South recording folk and blues singers in the early twentieth century.

Limeliters—but there is another dispiriting trend among the more militant young toward twisting insufficiently comprehended folk music into shrill weapons for "the cause." In an interview in *The Realist* [counterculture magazine] cartoonist Shel Silverstein tells of a Sunday experience in Washington Square: ". . . this one eighteen-year-old kid is sitting there with his guitar, and on the guitar is a sign that says, 'This Machine Fights for Freedom.' This is too much—an eighteen-year-old with a freedom-fighting machine. It's a goddam *guitar*, is what it is. It's a guitar, and it don't fight for nothing—it plays. Unless maybe . . . he hits with it."

On Folkways Records meanwhile there is a "freedom-fighting" singer, Bill McAdoo, who adds his own leaden lyrics to traditional tunes, and sings with a nearly total innocence of musical form or substance. The work song, *Jumping Judy*, becomes:

> I won't fight for Mr. Franco,
> Chiang Kai-shek or Syngman Rhee,
> I won't fight for Batista,
> I won't fight for tyranny.

I won't either, but even the prose of Max Lerner [political columnist known for his inspirational quotes] has somewhat more inspirational grace than Mr. McAdoo's stiff sloganeering. As the Gospel singing of the Southern Negro students has indicated (*We Shall Overcome*, Folkways), it's certainly possible to adapt folk material to current action; but the process usually is about as subtly executed as a *National Guardian* [conservative magazine] analysis of why Russia resumed [nuclear weapons] testing.

## From Immolation to Urbanization

Aside from this transmogrification of folk song into hoarse self-righteousness, there are the hopefully portentous artists among the new exploiters of the folk. Odetta, with a deep voice, choked diction, and as rigid a beat as [elderly TV host and bandleader] Lawrence Welk, has somehow captivated large numbers of undergraduates into confusing her with the Earth Mother. Except when he sings Jewish and some Russian songs, Theodore Bikel is also far from the marrow of the folk, but he at least doesn't regard his flair for entertainment as solemnly as Odetta, who seems to have picked up the idea that most folk songs were originally sung in a state of immolation.

There are a number of exceptions in the spread of juke box and "high art" folkum. A shy, stubborn, twenty-year-old from Boston, Joan Baez, has proved that even if Cecil Sharp [collector of English folk ballads in America] didn't collect some of his songs from her family, a singer with the imagination to penetrate folk music in a personal style that is luminously intense and meaningfully dramatic can contribute to a legitimate urbanization of the folk tradition. Miss Baez has occasional lapses of taste, but she is indeed an artist—one of the exceedingly few to have appeared among the non-indigenous folk performers. (*Joan Baez*, Vanguard).

In another direction, the New Lost City Ramblers have lovingly absorbed the spirit—as well as the pungent lyrics—of such mountain string groups of the late 1920's and early 1930's as Gid Tanner and his Skillet Lickers and Ernest Stoneman and his Blue Ridge Corn Shuckers. Theirs, to be sure, is a form of revivalism, but they know the backgrounds of the music and its original styles and have added their own brisk, high-spirited personalities. In short, their work is a tribute to their sources, not a theft from them. (*New Lost City Ramblers*, Folkways). In connection with the acquisitive approach to the folk tradition, there is the extraordinary grasping of copyright ownership to venerable ballads by the more prehensile performers. A case in point is a new Atlantic release of *The Golden Vanity* which appeared in one broadside version as early as 1682. The performer is Lonnie Donegan, a British young man who was once a guitarist in a quasi-jazz band. And the composer of *The Golden Vanity*—according to the record—is Lonnie Donegan.

Essentially, the most stimulating source of folk music is still the folk, or what's left of them; and the indefatigable editor-collector, Alan Lomax, continues to produce some of the most compelling authentic folk music on record. Having released a brilliantly illuminating *Southern Folk Heritage* (Atlantic), Lomax has more recently been represented as a reminder of the roots in Caedmon's three-volume *The Folksongs of Britain* (TC). The folkum tide, however, continues to rise. In early September, Grossinger's in the Catskills [upstate New York resort area] was the site of the first Annual Folk Music and Guitar Festival, which included a collegiate folk singing contest. Presumably, the contestant whose announcing style is closest to Jerry Lewis will be most likely to prove his right to the folkum crown.

# Bob Dylan Makes His New York Debut

## By Robert Shelton

Nineteen-year-old folksinger Bob Dylan arrived in New York City in January 1961 with visions of breaking into the flourishing folk music scene that had swept through the bars and coffeehouses of Greenwich Village, the city's bohemian enclave. By June, he had begun making regular appearances at music spots like the Gaslight, Café Wha?, and Gerde's Folk City. It was at Gerde's that Dylan first caught the attention of *New York Times* music critic Robert Shelton. Impressed by his stage presence and unique style, Shelton gave Dylan's career a huge boost by writing a review of his performances there for the September 29, 1961, edition of the *Times*. The favorable notice brought Dylan new fans and most likely helped him to secure a recording contract with Columbia Records by the close of 1961. From there, Dylan would soon go on to great acclaim, influencing the Beatles, the Rolling Stones, and the Byrds with songs of unsurpassed lyricism and originality.

In the following excerpt from Shelton's 1986 biography of Dylan, *No Direction Home*, the author recalls attending some of Dylan's earliest performances and the undeniable, though still nascent, talent that the young songwriter conveyed. Included is Shelton's *New York Times* review of Dylan, which notes Dylan's humorous and personalized approach to folk music.

I first encountered Dylan at a Monday night hoot [short for "hootenanny"—folk music jam sessions] at Folk City in June 1961. Because my reaction then to his performing was so strong, I know that I either never saw him at Folk City the previous April, or that I had looked right through him. At the hoot, Bob was doing his musical shaggy-dog story, "Bear Mountain," inspired by routines that Noel (Paul) Stookey, later of [successful 1960s pop group] Peter, Paul and Mary, was doing at the Gaslight.

## Discovering a New Talent

Bob looked like a European street singer or tumbler. He bobbed and swayed, played with his black corduroy Huck Finn cap, made faces, winced, and joked his way through the ridiculous narrative. I walked over to Pat Clancy, the Irish folk singer, and said: "Hey, Pat, you have to catch this kid!" Pat turned from his Jameson's whiskey and joined me to watch Bob. "Well, what have we here!" Pat exclaimed, half-curious and half-joyful. When the enthusiastic audience released Bob from the stage, I told him how much I liked his work. He appreciated my appreciation. "Yeah, great! I'm glad you liked it. I've done better sets than that. Glad you liked it," he said. I told him when he had his next job to call me and I'd try to review him in *The Times*. "I sure will, I sure will," he replied. "I think you missed me when I was here last April," Dylan said, and I admitted that I sure did, I sure did.

A week or two later, my phone rang and a thin, nasal voice said: "Hi, I'm Bob Dylan. You said I should call you if I got a job. Well, I got a job. I'm at the Gaslight for a week." Several days later I arrived at the Gaslight to see the regulars listening to [folksinger Dave] Van Ronk and Dylan. At his usual table in the rear was Albert B. Grossman, who appeared to be getting a great deal of satisfaction from a cup of coffee [and later became Dylan's manager]. In the early days, Albert often held court in coffeehouses. He usually smoked a king-size cigarette the way an oil sheik would hold a hookah, making a circle of his thumb and forefinger, slightly crooking his little finger, and blowing the smoke out slowly through his hand. I told Dylan the gig was too short to write up, but I introduced him to Albert, saying I thought this kid was going to be the next sensation. Grossman, as usual, said nothing. After Dylan left our table, Grossman asked what I thought of Van Ronk. I was enthusiastic but I predicted that Dy-

lan would go further. Grossman smiled, a Cheshire cat in untouched acres of field mice.

The Gaslight was then owned by a wild-looking Bohemian,
John Mitchell, who had fought many legal battles against police
and fire authorities who had cracked down on the MacDougal
Street coffeehouses. Mitchell found Dylan especially droll. Although Dylan was frequently nostalgic about the Gaslight, he
also made fun of his first job there. He once told me the Gaslight
was "the Broadway of folk song, where all the stars were—Dave
Van Ronk, [banjoist] Billy Faier, [balladeer] Hal Waters." His
Gaslight stint ended inconclusively. Grossman said nothing. I
hadn't written a word about him. Bob kept working at his music,
at his western speech. Sometimes his mangled dialect made
words virtually indistinguishable. He started to mumble about
"ramblin' and tumblin' with his coat collar turned up high." Soon,
a few of us were calling him "the rambler" and "the tumbler."

## Dylan's First Concert

Dylan rambled and tumbled into his first New York concert appearance and radio broadcast on Saturday, July 29, 1961. The
marathon was run by a new FM station, WRVR, operated by The
Riverside Church. To inaugurate the station's live-music project,
Izzy Young and Bob Yellin mobilized folk musicians. In those
days, at a call for folk talent, youngsters like Tom Paxton and
Molly Scott, and old-timers like the Reverend Gary Davis and
blues singer Victoria Spivey, would rush to perform, even without pay. WRVR's twelve-hour folk parade had enough lapses of
broadcasting techniques to gray an FCC [Federal Communications Commission] commissioner's head. On the hour every
hour, eager performers hit their mikes with swinging banjo
necks, voices faded in and out, cues were missed. The studio audience was as restless and partisan as a high-school assembly.

There were workshops on the blues, an Eastern Mediterranean
segment, and showcases for various banjo styles. No big-name
stars, but the show was an impressive display of available folk-
song and instrumental talent around town. Midway through the
afternoon, a slight musician who sang, looked, and twanged like
Woody Guthrie made his way to the microphone. Introduced as
hailing from Gallup, New Mexico, Dylan, with his harmonica
in a holder improvised from a metal coat hanger, was on for five
quick songs, joined on some by Jack Elliott and bluesman

Danny Kalb. In *The Times*, I briefly described Dylan's style as a "curiously arresting, mumbling, country-steeped manner." Dylan's little stint stimulated his coterie into enough noise to simulate a crowd.

After he left the stage, he was introduced to a seventeen-year-old, wide-eyed, long-haired beauty named Suze Rotolo, and began two years of an ecstatic, erratic romance. Dylan's reputation was growing as another Jack Elliott or Woody Guthrie [famed folksingers of the 1930s and 1940s], yet recording seemed the only doorway to national recognition. In late summer, a bright pair of Village girls, Sybil Weinberger, who worked in TV production, and Suze's older sister, Carla Rotolo, then personal assistant to Alan Lomax [musicologist who recorded many original folksingers], came up with an idea to help record Dylan and some other unknowns. They suggested a demonstration tape of half a dozen of the best Village folk singers, including Van Ronk and Elliott.

Describing the project and raving about Dylan in particular, Sybil wrote to producer John Hammond at Columbia Records. "Sybil's letter called attention to a whole group that had tremendous talent," Carla recalled. "By putting in people who had some recognition, we thought we might get some recognition for the unrecognized, like Bobby and John Wynn. But the original idea was to get Bobby something." There was no reply: Carla maintains Hammond just let the letter sit on his desk and may not even have read it. She thinks Hammond did not associate the Bobby Dylan in Sybil's letter and the boy he signed weeks later to a five-year Columbia contract.

## Two Weeks at Gerde's

Because of the urgings of the Dylan coterie in general, Carla in particular, and my interest in reviewing, Mike Porco [owner of Gerde's Folk City] booked Bob into Folk City again for two weeks: SEPTEMBER 25 THRU OCTOBER 8: GREENBRIAR BOYS, PICKING & SINGING THRU BLUEGRASS WITH THE SENSATIONAL BOB DYLAN. The Greenbriar Boys (Ralph Rinzler, John Herald, and Bob Yellin) were city bluegrass wizards. Yellin's banjo lines hopped around like confetti in the wind. Herald's vocal acrobatics keened in old-timey folk songs or in country burlesque, like "We Need a Whole Lot More of Jesus and a Lot Less Rock and Roll." Rinzler's delicate mandolin figures coursed like nervous birds nesting. All three sang and whooped it up with wit and musicianship. They were not an easy act to follow, but Dylan followed superbly.

During those two weeks, he alternated between three costumes, each seedier than the next. One outfit was a faded blue shirt, khaki trousers, a dark sleeveless pullover sweater, an incongruous foulard tie, all topped with his famous hat. Other nights he wore a chamois jacket or a tieless wool shirt. His Gibson guitar had a song-sequence sheet pasted on its upper curve, and his harmonica holder hung around his neck. He looked studiously unkempt and very slight and frail, until he began to sing. His pinched, constricted voice seemed to be fighting its way out of his throat. It was a rusty voice, suggesting Guthrie's old recordings. It was etched in gravel, like Van Ronk's. It sometimes crooned a bit, like Elliott's. Yet it was also a voice quite unlike anyone else's. You

*Bob Dylan*

didn't think of it as something beautiful or sinuous, but as something that roiled up from the heart. He didn't sound a bit citified, but more like a farmhand folk singer. Most of the audience liked Dylan those two weeks, regarding him as a masterly ethnic singer, but many thought he was just a bad joke.

Bob started a typical set with "I'm Gonna Get You, Sally Gal," in a lively tempo. He set up a three-way conversation between his voice, guitar, and mouth harp. Suddenly you saw how he could share the stage with as brilliant a trio as The Greenbriars. "Here's a song suitable to this occasion," Dylan said, as he retuned his guitar and changed his mouth harp. He sailed into a traditional blues dirge, "This Life Is Killing Me." His technique was everywhere, the covert technique of the folk idiom. It was antipolish, anticonscious of surface form, yet all those elements lay below. He gave the impression that he had started in music yesterday, not five years earlier. But one couldn't be sure.

Between songs, Dylan droned a soliloquy, formless yet very

funny. He started to tell a story about a toad. It was an open-ended shaggy-toad story that didn't start anyplace, didn't go anywhere, and didn't end anywhere, but it gave him a bit of fill-in patter while he tuned. His face was pouting and boyish. His slow delivery made him sound half-awake to optimists and half-asleep to pessimists. Next, he growled his way through "a train song," "900 Miles." To punctuate certain guitar breaks, he raised the body of his guitar to the microphone, an old country-music gambit that magnified the stringed sound.

In the background were the usual Folk City distractions. Bartenders clinked and poured as if starring in TV commercials. The cash register rang during soft passages. At the bar a few drunks were gabbing while others tried to silence them. Dylan was all concentration. "Here's a song outa my own head," he said, tuning his guitar for "Talking New York," a very old style of talking blues, in which three sparse chords support wry lyrics more spoken than sung. Dylan delivered his first protest song with a comic's timing.

Bob turned to other songs out of other people's heads. He moaned his way through "Dink's Song," long favored by Josh White and Cynthia Gooding; Dylan said he had picked it up on the Brazos River when he was down in Texas. Actually, the ballad hunter John A. Lomax had heard it in 1904 from a gin-drinking black woman who sang it as she wearily scrubbed her man's laundry. It is one of the most pathetic women's laments in American folk song. Bob did a variation on Van Ronk, with vamping guitar figures keeping the underlying pattern moving. At times his voice sounded like gravel being shoveled, at other times like a sob. He caught the original's tension, grit, and plaintiveness. "I was never a motherless child," folk singer Ed McCurdy used to say, "but I know what it feels like." Dylan was never a black laundress, but he knew what it felt like. Occasionally, Dylan threw his head back full as if he were scanning the ceiling for his next words.

From Texas, the twenty-year-old world traveler took his audience to a famous Chicago bar, Muddy Water's Place, where he said he had picked up another blues song. He shuffled to the junk-heap upright piano and played primitive chords. Then he hit Woody's road again, with "Hard Travelin'," a lurching, careening road song, sticky with hot asphalt, aching with calloused feet. Then he did another couple of songs out of his own head, including "Bear Mountain" and "Talkin' Hava Negilah Blues,"

his little jape of international "stylists" like Harry Belafonte and
Theo Bikel.

The audience responded more to Dylan's wit than to his slow,
serious, intense material. Audience reaction led him to play
Chaplinesque clown. He closed with his own "Song to Woody,"
suspensefully built to keep attention focused on each new line.

## "Putting On" His Interviewer

After his set, we went back to the Folk City kitchen for his first
press interview. The answers came fast, but I had a feeling that
he was improvising and concealing. It went like this: "I'm twenty
years old, don't turn twenty-one until May. I've been singing all
my life, since I was ten. I was born in Duluth, Minnesota, or
maybe it was Superior, Wisconsin, right across the line. I started
traveling with a carnival at the age of thirteen. I did odd jobs and
sang with the carnival. I cleaned up ponies and ran steam shov-
els, in Minnesota, North Dakota, and then on south. I graduated
from high school. For a while, Sioux Falls, South Dakota, was a
home, and so was Gallup, New Mexico. I also lived in Fargo,
North Dakota, and in a place called Hibbing, Minnesota. I went
to the University of Minnesota for about eight months, but I did-
n't like it too much. I used to play piano with Bobby Vee and The
Shadows, a country rockabilly band. I came east in February
1961, and it's just as hard as any town I've seen."

When he sang "Poor Girl," he had pulled out a kitchen table
knife and used the back of the blade to fret his guitar. Where did
he learn that old blues bottleneck guitar? "I learned to use a
butcher knife," Bob replied, "from an old guy named Wigglefoot
in Gallup, New Mexico. He was a beaten-down old bluesman
who wore a patch on his eye. I do a lot of material I learned from
Mance Lipscomb, but not in public. Mance was a big influence.
I met him in Navasota, Texas, five years ago. I've been a farmhand too. I learned 'House of the Rising Sun' from Dave Van
Ronk and 'See That My Grave Is Kept Clean' from Blind Lemon
Jefferson. I like the recordings of Rabbit Brown a lot too.

"Jack Elliott and Dave Van Ronk are the two best folk singers
in New York. I can only sing one way . . . in the way I like to hear
it. I don't have a pretty voice. I can't sing pretty, and I don't want
to sing pretty." Bob dropped the names of a lot of admired musicians, a mélange of those he had heard on recordings only and
those he said he'd met and worked with. He appeared to have

known them all. "Yes, I like Ray Charles very much. I picked up the harmonica after hearing Walter Jacobs—you know, Little Walter—of the Muddy Waters band. But I play my own style of harmonica. I played piano for dancers in the carnival."

Had he made any recordings? "The recordings I've made haven't been released. I played with Gene Vincent in Nashville, but I don't know if they have been released. . . . As to that bottleneck guitar, when I played a coffeehouse in Detroit I used a switchblade knife to get that sound. But when I pulled out the switchblade, six people in the audience walked out. They looked afraid. Now, I just use a kitchen knife so no one will walk out." Any other musical influences? "A lot, quite a lot. Woody Guthrie, of course. I have seen quite a lot of Woody since last winter. We can talk, even though he is sick [Guthrie was dying of Huntington's disease at the time]. He likes my songs a lot. I met Jesse Fuller two years ago in Denver and studied with him."

Bob went on for another set. I told Carla that it had been a good interview and that I really loved his work and manner. But, I told her, I had the strange feeling he was putting me on. He seemed to have traveled so far and known so many famous and obscure musicians. He was evasive about his past. I told Carla to tell Bob there was a difference between kidding around with a Village guy and talking for publication. Minutes after Dylan's set Carla huddled with Bobby, and then we continued the interview at a table in between songs by The Greenbriar Boys.

## Reviewed in the *New York Times*

"Listen," Bob told me, "I'm giving it to you straight. I wouldn't tell you anything that isn't true." Did he want me to call him Bobby Dylan or Bob Dylan? He thought that one out, as if he were about to sign a contract. Half aloud, he repeated the two names to himself: "Bob Dylan, Bobby Dylan, Bob Dylan, Bobby Dylan . . . Make it Bob Dylan! That's what I'm really known as," he declared confidently. I wrote the review, which appeared in *The Times* on Friday, September 29, 1961:

A bright new face in folk music is appearing at Gerde's Folk City. Although only 20 years old, Bob Dylan is one of the most distinctive stylists to play in a Manhattan cabaret in months.

Resembling a cross between a choir boy and a beatnik, Mr. Dylan has a cherubic look and a mop of tousled hair he partly covers with a Huck Finn black corduroy cap. His clothes may need a bit of tailoring, but when he works his guitar, harmonica or piano and composes new songs faster than he can remember them, there is no doubt that he is bursting at the seams with talent. Mr. Dylan's voice is anything but pretty. He is consciously trying to recapture the rude beauty of a Southern field hand musing in melody on his back porch. All the "husk and bark" are left on his notes, and a searing intensity pervades his songs.

Mr. Dylan is both comedian and tragedian. Like a vaudeville actor on the rural circuit, he offers a variety of droll musical monologues. "Talking Bear Mountain" lampoons the overcrowding of an excursion boat. "Talking New York" satirizes his troubles in gaining recognition and "Talkin' Hava Negilah" burlesques the folk-music craze and the singer himself. In his serious vein, Mr. Dylan seems to be performing in a slow-motion film. Elasticized phrases are drawn out until you think they may snap. He rocks his head and body. He closes his eyes in reverie, seems to be groping for a word or a mood, then resolves the tension benevolently by finding the word and the mood. He may mumble the text of "House of the Rising Sun" in a scarcely understandable growl, or sob, or clearly enunciate the poetic poignancy of a Blind Lemon Jefferson blues, "One kind favor I ask of you—See that my grave is kept clean."

Mr. Dylan's highly personalized approach toward folk song is still evolving. He has been sopping up influences like a sponge. At times, the drama he aims at is off-target melodrama and his stylization threatens to topple over as a mannered excess. But if not for every taste, his music-making has the mark of originality and inspiration, all the more noteworthy for his youth. Mr. Dylan is vague about his antecedents and birthplace, but it matters less where he has been than where he is going, and that would seem to be straight up. . . .

This was followed by four laudatory paragraphs about The Greenbriar Boys. As good as they were, Dylan seemed to be the news. By chance, the entertainment section had a canyon at the top of one review page. Across three columns ran the headline: BOB DYLAN: A DISTINCTIVE STYLIST. A rough photo of Dylan with his hat, his tie, and his big guitar got three inches of space. The layout, the picture, and the headline trumpeted Dylan even louder than my story.

## Jealous Carping, New Fans, and a Recording Contract

Reactions couldn't have varied more. A very few musicians were pleased. Elliott read the notice aloud in his best Dylanesque voice to a few drinkers at the Dugout on Bleecker Street. Van Ronk, cool but gulping hard, told me I had done "a very, very fine thing." Pat Clancy and his brother, Tom, said, "Bobby has a lot of talent. He deserves to go places." Izzy Young said he had discovered Dylan months earlier than anyone. And much of the Village music coterie reacted with jealousy, contempt, and ridicule. Eric Weissberg and Marshall Brickman, two of the ablest instrumentalists about, told me I needed a hearing aid. Logan English, a singer who had suffered inordinate difficulties getting his own career moving, was sarcastic and rueful. To a man, The Greenbriar Boys were hurt that this "kid" had eclipsed them. Bob Yellin didn't talk to me for weeks. Fred Hellerman, a songwriter and arranger, formerly of The Weavers, was openly derisive: "How on earth can you say that he is such a great this-and-that?" he asked me on a street corner. "He can't sing, and he can barely play, and he doesn't know much about music at all. I think you've gone off the deep end!" Manny Greenhill, [Boston folksinger Joan] Baez's kindly manager, said my review was "talking about Bobby in a year or two, not now." Charlie Rothschild said he saw some potential in Dylan "but he's got a long way to go." Most enthusiastic, however, were Carolyn [Hester, another Boston-based folksinger] and Richard Fariña. They were delighted because they liked Bob, personally and musically, and because he was scheduled to play on Carolyn's upcoming recording.

Dylan showed up at Folk City that Friday night pale and shaken. There was a very big turnout. As he walked in, patrons turned to each other and said: "There he is! That's the guy!" Bob looked uncertain that he could deliver, now that the order had been placed. He thanked me warmly and began his long years of telling me, "You're a very good writer, not just music, but a very good writer." Through twenty years of reviewing, I can recall no other performer who seemed more concerned about a reviewer's feelings. When he was spinning out of orbit, Dylan lashed out at me for things I wrote, but those moments were exceptions. From the start, he knew that writers are as hungry for applause as musicians.

That fourth night of his gig, Bob had an even more engrossed audience. One stranger at the bar puzzled us. He was fiftyish, moon-faced, well dressed, smiled a great deal, and offered drinks to some of the kids who knew Dylan. Bob passed the word quickly: "Fuzz!" Much later he described the man as one of the many police who "followed" him. "He was a cop," Bob said later. "I told you about that at the time. Why, cops have been following me all my life. Cops haven't been following me much after 1964, but until then they used to come from all over." No one ever found out who the wicked messenger was that night.

Later in the evening, Dylan steered me to a quiet corner and said: "I don't want you to tell anybody about this, but I saw John Hammond, Sr., this afternoon and he offered me a five-year contract with Columbia! But, please, man, keep it quiet because it won't be definite until Monday. I met him at Carolyn's session today. I shook his hand with my right hand and I gave him your review with my left hand. He offered to sign me without even hearing me sing! But don't tell anyone, not one single soul! It could get messed up by someone at the top of Columbia, but I think it is really going to happen. Five years on Columbia! How do you like that?"

# U.S. Involvement in Vietnam Deepens

## By Dean Rusk and Robert S. McNamara

U.S. military involvement in the defense of South Vietnam against a Communist takeover grew significantly throughout 1961. Guerrillas from Communist North Vietnam, known as the Viet Cong, had infiltrated the South and were destabilizing President Ngo Dinh Diem's regime. Meanwhile, Soviet-backed forces had largely succeeded in installing a Communist regime in Laos, which bordered Vietnam. President John F. Kennedy's advisers warned him that the nations of Southeast Asia were vulnerable to a "domino effect" in which communism would rapidly spread throughout the region as one after another democratic regime fell.

The following November 11, 1961, memorandum to the president from Secretary of State Dean Rusk and Secretary of Defense Robert S. McNamara demonstrates how the defense of South Vietnam had become a primary objective of Kennedy's foreign policy by the fall of 1961. They recommend that Kennedy "commit [himself] to the clear objective of preventing the fall of South Viet-Nam to Communists," and insist that the use of combat troops may become necessary to "strike at the source of aggression in North Viet-Nam." Reluctant to send in combat troops, Kennedy largely followed these recommendations and increased the number of U.S. military advisers in South Vietnam from eight hundred to sixteen thousand by the end of the year. Most important, the president made it clear to allies in the region that he would not tolerate another Communist victory in Southeast Asia.

Dean Rusk and Robert S. McNamara, "Memorandum for the President, November 11, 1961," *United States–Vietnam Relations: 1945–1967*. Washington, DC: U.S. Government Printing Office, 1971.

The stage had been set for the Vietnam War.

Dean Rusk was the U.S. secretary of state from 1961 to 1969, and Robert S. McNamara was the U.S. secretary of defense from 1961 to 1968. Both men served in the administrations of Kennedy and his successor, President Lyndon B. Johnson.

## United States National Interests in South Viet-Nam

The deteriorating situation in South Viet-Nam requires attention to the nature and scope of United States national interests in that country. The loss of South Viet-Nam to Communism would involve the transfer of a nation of 20 million people from the free world to the Communist bloc. The loss of South Viet-Nam would make pointless any further discussion about the importance of Southeast Asia to the free world; we would have to face the near certainty that the remainder of Southeast Asia and Indonesia would move to a complete accommodation with Communism, if not formal incorporation within the Communist bloc. The United States, as a member of SEATO [Southeast Asia Treaty Organization, formed in 1954], has commitments with respect to South Viet-Nam under the Protocol to the SEATO Treaty. Additionally, in a formal statement at the conclusion session of the 1954 Geneva Conference [on Indochina, which resulted in the Geneva Accords partitioning Vietnam at the 17th parallel], the United States representative stated that the United States "would view any renewal of the aggression . . . with grave concern and seriously threatening international peace and security."

The loss of South Viet-Nam to Communism would not only destroy SEATO but would undermine the credibility of American commitments elsewhere. Further, loss of South Viet-Nam would stimulate bitter domestic controversies in the United States and would be seized upon by extreme elements to divide the country and harass the Administration.

## The Problem of Saving South Viet-Nam

It seems, on the face of it, absurd to think that a nation of 20 million people can be subverted by 15–20 thousand active guerrillas [the Communist Viet Cong] if the Government and people of that country do not wish to be subverted. South Viet-Nam is not, however, a highly organized society with an effective governing apparatus and a population accustomed to carrying civic responsibility. Public apathy is encouraged by the inability of most citizens to act directly as well as by the tactics of terror employed by the guerrillas throughout the countryside. Inept administration and the absence of a strong non-Communist political coalition have made it difficult to bring available resources to bear upon the guerrilla problem and to make the most effective use of available external aid. Under the best of conditions the threat posed by the presence of 15–20 thousand guerrillas, well disciplined under well-trained cadres, would be difficult to meet.

## The United States' Objective in South Viet-Nam

*The United States should commit itself to the clear objective of preventing the fall of South Viet-Nam to Communists.* The basic means for accomplishing this objective must be to put the Government of South Viet-Nam [led by authoritarian president Ngo Dinh Diem from 1954 to 1963] into a position to win its own war against the guerrillas. We must insist that that Government itself take the measures necessary for that purpose in exchange for large-scale United States assistance in the military, economic and political fields. At the same time we must recognize that it will probably not be possible for the GVN [Government of Viet-Nam] to win this war as long as the flow of men and supplies from [Communist] North Viet-Nam continues unchecked and the guerrillas enjoy a safe sanctuary in neighboring territory.

We should be prepared to introduce United States combat forces if that should become necessary for success. Dependent upon the circumstances, it may also be necessary for United States forces to strike at the source of the aggression in North Viet-Nam.

## The Use of United States Forces in South Viet-Nam

The commitment of United States forces to South Viet-Nam involves two different categories: (A) Units of modest size required for the direct support of South Viet-Namese military effort, such as communications, helicopter and other forms of airlift, reconnaissance aircraft, naval patrols, intelligence units, etc., and (B) larger organized units with actual or potential direct military missions. *Category (A) should be introduced as speedily as possible.* Category (B) units pose a more serious problem in that they are much more significant from the point of view of domestic and international political factors and greatly increase the probabilities of Communist bloc escalation. Further, the employment of United States combat forces (in the absence of Communist bloc escalation) involves a certain dilemma: if there is a strong South-Vietnamese effort, they may not be needed; if there is not such an effort, United States forces could not accomplish their mission in the midst of an apathetic or hostile population. Under present circumstances, therefore, the question of injecting United States and SEATO combat forces should in large part be considered as a contribution to the morale of the South Viet-Namese in their own effort to do the principal job themselves.

## Probable Extent of the Commitment of United States Forces

If we commit Category (B) forces to South Viet-Nam, the ultimate possible extent of our military commitment in Southeast Asia must be faced. The struggle may be prolonged, and Hanoi [the capital of North Viet-Nam] and Peiping [Beijing, the capital of Communist China] may overtly intervene. It is the view of the Secretary of Defense and the Joint Chiefs of Staff that, in the light of the logistic difficulties faced by the other side, we can assume that the maximum United States forces required on the ground in Southeast Asia would not exceed six divisions, or about 205,000 men (CINCPAC Plan 32/59 PHASE IV). This would be in addition to local forces and such SEATO forces as may be engaged. It is also the view of the Secretary of Defense and the Joint Chiefs of Staff that our military posture is, or, with the addition of more National Guard or regular Army divisions, can be made, adequate to furnish these forces and support them in action without serious interference with our present Berlin plans.

## Relation to Laos

It must be understood that the introduction of American combat forces into Viet-Nam prior to a Laotian settlement would run a considerable risk of stimulating a Communist breach of the cease fire and a resumption of hostilities in Laos. This could present us with a choice between the use of combat forces in Laos or an abandonment of that country to full Communist control. At the present time, there is at least a chance that a settlement can be reached in Laos on the basis of a weak and unsatisfactory Souvanna Phouma Government. The prospective agreement on Laos includes a provision that Laos will not be used as a transit area or as a base for interfering in the affairs of other countries such as South Viet-Nam. After a Laotian settlement, the introduction of United States forces into Viet-Nam could serve to stabilize the position both in Viet-Nam and in Laos by registering our determination to see to it that the Laotian settlement was as far as the United States would be willing to see Communist influence in Southeast Asia develop.

## The Need for Multilateral Action

From the political point of view, both domestic and international, it would seem important to involve forces from other nations alongside of United States Category (B) forces in Viet-Nam. It would be difficult to explain to our own people why no effort had been made to invoke SEATO or why the United States undertook to carry this burden unilaterally. Our position would be greatly strengthened if the introduction of forces could be taken as a

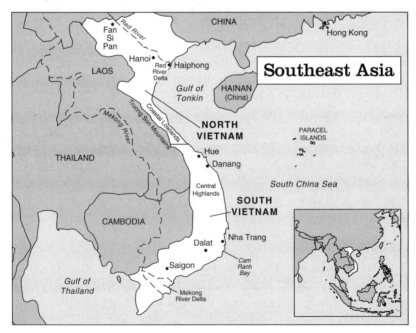

SEATO action, accompanied by units of other SEATO countries, with a full SEATO report to the United Nations of the purposes of the action itself.

Apart from the armed forces, there would be political advantage in enlisting the interest of other nations, including neutrals, in the security and well-being of South Viet-Nam. This might be done by seeking such assistance as Malayan police officals. . . and by technical assistance personnel in other fields, either bilaterally or through international organizations.

## Initial Diplomatic Action by the United States

If the recommendations, below, are approved, the United States should consult intensively with other SEATO governments to obtain their full support of the course of action contemplated. At the appropriate stage, a direct approach should be made by the United States to Moscow, through normal or special channels, pointing out that we cannot accept the movement of cadres, arms and other supplies into South Viet-Nam in support of the guerrillas. We should also discuss the problem with neutral governments in the general area and get them to face up to their own interests in the security of South Viet-Nam; these governments will be concerned about (a) the introduction of United States combat forces and (b) the withdrawal of United States support from Southeast Asia; their concern, therefore, might be usefully expressed either to Communist bloc countries or in political support for what may prove necessary in South Viet-Nam itself.

## Recommendations

In the light of the foregoing, the Secretary of State and the Secretary of Defense recommend that:

1. We now take the decision to commit ourselves to the objective of preventing the fall of South Viet-Nam to Communism and that, in doing so, we recognize that the introduction of United States and other SEATO forces may be necessary to achieve this objective. (However, if it is necessary to commit outside forces to achieve the foregoing objective our decision to introduce United States forces should not be contingent upon unanimous SEATO agreement thereto.)

2. The Department of Defense be prepared with plans for the use of United States forces in South Viet-Nam under one or more of the following purposes:

(a) Use of a significant number of United States forces to signify United States determination to defend South Viet-Nam and to boost South Viet-Nam morale.

(b) Use of substantial United States forces to assist in suppressing Viet Cong insurgency short of engaging in detailed counter-guerrilla operations but including relevant operations in North Viet-Nam.

(c) Use of United States forces to deal with the situation if there is organized Communist military intervention.

3. We immediately undertake the following actions in support of the GVN:

(a) Provide increased air lift to the GVN forces, including helicopters, light aviation, and transport aircraft, manned to the extent necessary by United States uniformed personnel and under United States operational control.

(b) Provide such additional equipment and United States uniformed personnel as may be necessary for air reconnaissance, photography, instruction in and execution of air-ground support techniques, and for special intelligence.

(c) Provide the GVN with small craft, including such United States uniformed advisers and operating personnel as may be necessary for quick and effective operations in effecting surveillance and control over coastal waters and inland waterways.

(d) Provide expedited training and equipping of the civil guard and the self-defense corps with the objective of relieving the regular Army of static missions and freeing it for mobile offensive operations.

(e) Provide such personnel and equipment as may be necessary to improve the military-political intelligence system beginning at the provincial level and extending upward through the Government and the armed forces to the Central Intelligence Organization.

(f) Provide such new terms of reference, reorganization and additional personnel for United States military forces as are required for increased United States participation in the direction and control of GVN military operations and to carry out the other increased responsibilities which accrue to MAAG under these recommendations.

(g) Provide such increased economic aid as may be required to permit the GVN to pursue a vigorous flood relief [South Viet-Nam had experienced severe flooding during the spring 1961 monsoon season] and rehabilitation program, to supply material in support of the security effort, and to give priority to projects in support of this expanded counter-insurgency program. (This could include increases in military pay, a full supply of a wide range of materials such as food, medical supplies, transportation equipment, communications equipment, and any other items where material help could assist the GVN in winning the war against the Viet Cong.)

(h) Encourage and support (including financial support) a request by the GVN to the FAO or any other appropriate international organization for multilateral assistance in the relief and rehabilitation of the flood area.

(i) Provide individual administrators and advisers for insertion into the Governmental machinery of South Viet-Nam in types and numbers to be agreed upon by the two Governments.

(j) Provide personnel for a joint survey with the GVN of conditions in each of the provinces to assess the social, political, intelligence, and military factors bearing on the prosecution of the counter-insurgency program in order to reach a common estimate of these factors and a common determination of how to deal with them.

4. Ambassador Nolting [U.S. ambassador to South Viet-Nam] be instructed to make an immediate approach to President Diem to the effect that the Government of the United States is prepared to join the Government of Viet-Nam in a sharply increased joint effort to cope with the Viet Cong threat and the ravages of the flood as set forth under 3., above, if, on its part, the Government of Viet-Nam is prepared to carry out an effective and total mobilization of its own resources, both material and human, for the same end. Before setting in motion the United States proposals listed above, the United States Government would appreciate confirmation of their acceptability to the GVN, and an expression from the GVN of the undertakings it is prepared to make to insure the success of this joint effort. On the part of the United States, it would be expected that these GVN undertakings would include, in accordance with the detailed recommendations of the [General Maxwell] Taylor Mission and the Country Team:

(a) Prompt and appropriate legislative and administrative action to put the nation on a wartime footing to mobilize its entire resources. (This would include a decentralization and broadening of the Government so as to realize the full potential of all non-Communist elements in the country willing to contribute to the common struggle.)

(b) The establishment of appropriate Governmental wartime agencies with adequate authority to perform their functions effectively.

(c) Overhaul of the military establishment and command structure so as to create an effective military organization for the prosecution of the war.

5. Very shortly before the arrival in South Viet-Nam of the first increments of United States military personnel and equipment proposed under 3., above, that would exceed the Geneva Accord ceilings, publish the "Jordan report" [name for report *A Threat to Peace: North Viet-Nam Effort to Conquer South Viet-Nam* released on December 8, 1961] as a United States "white paper," transmitting it as simultaneously as possible to the Goverments of all countries with which we have diplomatic relations, including the Communist states.

6. Simultaneous with the publication of the "Jordan report," release an exchange of letters between Diem and the President [John F. Kennedy].

(a) Diem's letter would include: reference to the DRV [Democratic Republic of Viet-Nam, or North Viet-Nam] violations of Geneva Accords as set forth in the October 24 GVN letter to the ICC [International Control Commission] and other documents; pertinent references to GVN statements with respect to its intent to observe the Geneva Accords; reference to its need for flood relief and rehabilitation; reference to previous United States aid and the compliance hitherto by both countries with the Geneva Accords; reference to the USG statement at the time the Geneva Accords were signed; the necessity now of exceeding some provisions of the Accords in view of the DRV violations thereof; the lack of aggressive intent with respect to the DRV: GVN intent to return to strict compliance with the Geneva Accords as soon as the DRV violations ceased; and request for additional United States assistance in framework foregoing policy. The letter should also set forth in appropriate general terms steps Diem has taken and is taking to reform Governmental structure.

(b) The President's reply would be responsive to Diem's request for additional assistance and acknowledge and agree to Diem's statements on the intent promptly to return to strict compliance with the Geneva Accords as soon as DRV violations have ceased.

7. Simultaneous with steps 5 and 6, above, make a private approach to the Soviet Union that would include: our determination to prevent the fall of South Viet-Nam to Communism by whatever means is necessary; our concern over dangers to peace presented by the aggressive DRV policy with respect to South Viet-Nam; our intent to return to full compliance with the Geneva Accords as soon as the DRV does so; the distinction we draw between Laos and South Viet-Nam; and our expectation that the Soviet Union will exercise its influence on the CHICOMS [Chinese Communists] and the DRV.

8. A special diplomatic approach made to the United Kingdom in its role as co-Chairman of the Geneva Conference requesting that the United Kingdom seek the support of the Soviet co-Chairman for a cessation of DRV aggression against South Viet-Nam.

9. A special diplomatic approach also to be made to India, both in its role as Chairman of the ICC and as a power having relations with Peiping and Hanoi. This approach should be made immediately prior to public release of the "Jordan report" and the exchange of letters between Diem and the President.

10. Immediately prior to the release of the "Jordan report" and the exchange of letters between Diem and the President, special diplomatic approaches also to be made to Canada, as well as Burma, Indonesia, Cambodia, Ceylon, the UAR, and Yugoslavia. SEATO, NATO [North Atlantic Treaty Organization], and OAS [Organization of American States] members should be informed through those organizations, with selected members also informed individually. The possibility of some special approach to Poland as a member of the ICC should also be considered.

# Enlarging the Battle for Civil Rights: Mass Demonstrations in the South

### By *U.S. News & World Report*

On December 12, 1961, the Reverend Martin Luther King Jr., led several hundred protesters to the Albany, Georgia, city hall where eleven Freedom Riders had been jailed two days earlier for violating city ordinances at the train station. Begun in May 1961, the Freedom Rides were a series of ongoing protests intended to challenge the segregation of black passengers in the buses, trains, and transportation terminals of the South. King and the marchers were soon jailed for refusing to disperse, and more than seven hundred demonstrators were eventually arrested. That same week, seventy-three black college students were arrested in Baton Rouge, Louisiana, during a protest against segregated lunch counters that had attracted nearly two thousand participants.

The sheer size of these protests pointed to the impatience of certain activists, both black and white, to bring change to the South; however, the strategy of a "mass attack" on segregation had its detractors within the civil rights movement. In the following article on the protests, reporters from *U.S. News & World Report* quote a spokesman from the

"New Turn in Race Troubles," *U.S. News & World Report*, vol. 52, January 1, 1962, p. 43.

National Association for the Advancement of Colored People (NAACP), a pioneering civil rights group, who complains that the same issues could have been raised with a handful of demonstrators. In addition, he asserts that paying the legal bills of hundreds of jailed protesters is a huge strain on the NAACP's limited budget. This rift over the best strategy for winning black rights in America would foment the rise of the Black Power movement in the later years of the 1960s, as young blacks grew disenchanted with the slow progress of established groups like the NAACP.

S uddenly, in mid-December [1961], the Negro fight against racial segregation took a new turn.

Negroes by the hundreds began marching through the streets of one Southern city after another in mass demonstrations of protest.

First it was Albany, Ga. There, on December 12, a march by 400 Negroes set off a series of demonstrations that wound up with 700 Negroes in jail. Then, on December 15, nearly 2,000 Negroes staged a march in Baton Rouge, La. Police broke it up with tear gas, arrested 73. Three days later, on December 18, nearly 300 Negroes were arrested while they were trying to march through New Orleans.

Negro demonstrations of such size had not been seen before in the South.

What was happening?

## A New Strategy

Soon, from Negro leaders, came this answer: A new strategy for the war against segregation is being tried.

The strategy, in effect, is one of "mass attack." It calls for mass challenges of segregation practices. Instead of sending a few—or a few dozen—Negroes out to create a test case, as in the past, the new idea is to send out several hundred—or several thousand.

For these demonstrations, college students are preferred. High-school students are considered too excitable, older people too cautious. But the main idea is to parade in large numbers.

One Negro leader explained:

"We found that, if a few young people demonstrate, they usually are called agitators. But if a large crowd of youths turns out, they often are looked upon, even by whites, as patriots."

Behind this new strategy is the Congress of Racial Equality, known as CORE, an organization with headquarters in New York City.

CORE officials describe their strategy as one of "militant non-violence."

James L. Farmer, CORE's national director, expects the strategy to spread. He predicts that in the future there will be "more people getting involved in nonviolent demonstrations, more people going to jail."

## "Free in '63"

Travel through the South and you find, among Negroes, a changing mood. Their confidence is growing. And, as their confidence grows, they become more militant and more willing to go all out on a mass demonstration.

The new cry being shouted by Negroes is "Free in '63," expressing the Negro hope that by 1963 their fight against segregation will be won.

Many Negroes expect that President Kennedy will strike the deciding blow in their fight by issuing "a new Emancipation Proclamation" calling for the end of segregation in all its forms.

A common prediction is that Mr. Kennedy will issue such a proclamation on Jan. 1, 1963—the 100th anniversary of the date on which Abraham Lincoln freed the slaves. But some Negroes think the President may issue it even earlier—in the congressional-election year of 1962.

In spite of the gains that are being made by Negroes in eliminating racial barriers, all is not happiness within the Negro community.

For one thing, Negro organizations are disputing over strategy.

On one side, urging "mass attacks," is CORE. The Southern Christian Leadership Conference [SCLC], led by the Rev. Martin Luther King, Jr., and the Students' Nonviolent Co-ordinating Committee [SNCC] also employ this strategy.

On the other side, opposing the strategy of "mass attack," is the National Association for the Advancement of Colored People—the NAACP.

The NAACP, which once was regarded by white segregationists as the major source of their troubles, is now emerging as a comparatively conservative organization.

One person familiar with Negro attitudes reported a growing apprehension that CORE may be pushing too hard and too fast. He said:

"Conservative Negroes are worried that mass demonstrations, although they may produce dramatic gains, may provoke dramatic reactions."

## Expensive Strategy

NAACP leaders admit publicly that the mass demonstrations—and the mass arrests that follow them—are putting a severe strain on the NAACP budget.

Nearly every time a CORE demonstration lands a Negro in jail, that Negro looks to the NAACP to get him out, because the NAACP is the group handling most of the Negroes' legal battles. It has a special fund for that purpose.

When arrests multiply, legal costs also multiply.

Roy Wilkins, executive secretary of the NAACP, estimates that legal costs for the "Freedom Riders" and other demonstrators arrested in 1961 might run as high as a million dollars.

One CORE leader was quoted as saying on arrival at the scene of a recent demonstration: "We have got to get a lot of people arrested right away."

The NAACP sees no point in seeking mass arrests. NAACP leaders emphasize that they agree with CORE's aims. But they ask:

"Why make an issue of 300 people when the same legal principle can be established by three?"

## Who Won in Albany?

Questions also are being raised about the efficacy of the mass demonstrations.

In Albany, Ga., for example, the "mass attack" ended in a truce between Negro leaders and city officials. By the terms of the December 18 truce, the Negroes agreed to a 60-day moratorium on demonstrations—including boycotts—and to wait approximately a month before pressing for further negotiations.

City officials agreed to free the arrested demonstrators on low bonds, with property owners permitted to sign their own bonds—all with the understanding that the cases might never be pressed if all goes quietly.

As for the goal of the demonstrations: City officials agreed to let Negroes use bus and train terminals freely—but the restaurants in the terminals remained segregated.

Many Albany Negroes saw no real gains in the settlement. A few Negroes had previously used depot facilities without interference.

Albany whites claimed a clear victory. The chief of police, Laurie Pritchett, said: "We have met nonviolence with nonviolence, and we are happy with the results."

Chief Pritchett was widely praised for the way he handled the mass marches without any interracial violence.

Some of the Negro demonstrators reportedly went around the streets saying: "I love you, God loves you. Hit me. Hit me." But nobody was hit.

The split within Negro ranks over strategy was quite apparent in Albany.

Many Negroes here expressed criticism of Dr. King, who dashed to Albany after the demonstrations began and was arrested.

In spite of the unusual size of the demonstrations, only a very small proportion of Albany's 25,000 Negroes took part. The collection plate was passed around repeatedly, but only about $400 was collected for the Negro cause.

Dr. King went back to Atlanta as soon as he got out of jail.

## A Setback in Court

On the same day that Negroes in Albany were settling for a truce—December 18—the U.S. Supreme Court in Washington handed down a ruling that added to the problems of Negro demonstrators.

The Supreme Court refused to order a temporary halt in the prosecution of "Freedom Riders" in Jackson, Miss., where more than 300 have been arrested.

That decision did not in any way imply judicial approval of the Jackson prosecutions. It only questioned the qualification of the three plaintiffs to speak for all the defendants.

Effect of the decision, however, is to compel each Negro arrested to fight his own long and costly battle through the complicated process of trial and appeal—instead of settling many cases at once in a group action.

A week earlier, on December 11, the Supreme Court had set aside convictions of 16 Negro students charged with disturbing the peace by sitting in at Baton Rouge lunch counters that are traditionally reserved for whites.

In that decision, however, the Court merely ruled that the evidence was insufficient to support the verdict—and avoided any ruling on the important constitutional issues involved.

Some legal authorities see in the Supreme Court's recent rulings a growing disinclination to reach out for a constitutional issue in cases involving Negroes. These authorities foresee, as a result, possible slowdown in the pace of integration by court decree.

Still to be settled by the nation's highest tribunal are such constitutional questions as whether a private business owner has a right to refuse to serve Negroes and whether sit-in demonstrators can be convicted under trespass laws.

This leaves still in doubt the question of whether courts can be used by Negroes to eliminate segregation practices in private business.

Meanwhile, an increasingly militant group of Negro leaders is determined to press ahead with "mass attacks" against segregation on all fronts.

This new strategy can be expected to produce some more big and dramatic demonstrations in the South.

# American Youth: The Pampered Generation

## By George Gallup and Evan Hill

In December 1961 researcher George Gallup and his assistant Evan Hill published the results of an extensive survey they had conducted on the opinions and aspirations of the "typical" American youth for the *Saturday Evening Post*, a popular weekly magazine. Gallup was the founder and director of the American Institute of Public Opinion, an organization that introduced the Gallup Poll—a method of polling and statistical analysis—to explore public opinion on a variety of issues. As the following analysis of the survey indicates, the nation's young were largely a product of the postwar prosperity that had enabled many families to reach unprecedented levels of affluence. Gallup and Hill reveal a pampered generation of young people with little interest in politics or the world outside their cocoons of prosperity. Notable exceptions to the general apathy—the researchers describe a "vigorous minority" of young people who had taken an active role in social justice and politics—clearly existed, but by the end of 1961, the nation had yet to stumble upon the "rallying point" that would soon ignite its youth to widespread political activism.

George Gallup and Evan Hill, "Youth: The Cool Generation," *Saturday Evening Post*, vol. 234, December 23–30, 1961, pp. 64–80. Copyright © 1961 by *Saturday Evening Post*. Reproduced by permission.

**W**hat is the average—or typical—American youth? How can we find him, and when we do, what meaning does he have? He is, of course, important. Down through the ages, adults have judged the future by the current crop of youth. Depending on their views, they have voiced hope or despair as youth matured and was harvested into manhood. And usually their judgment was wrong, distorted by middle-aged myopia and nostalgic memories of a bygone youth that never really was and never really is. They have judged a generation by the boy in the living room and the boy next door, and their observation was too limited.

## Dissecting American Youth

Now, with the advantages of scientific fact finding, a nation may move out of the living room and into the land, examining its youth as individuals and as groups, uncovering what is truly typical. Some months ago the editors of *The Saturday Evening Post* commissioned us to dissect and reassemble American youth, using the facilities of the Gallup Poll, Since then we have interviewed more than 3000 young Americans ranging in age from fourteen through twenty-two. We asked each one more than 200 questions. Our sample included 648 high-school sophomores, 641 high-school seniors, 1020 juniors and seniors from seventy-eight American colleges, and 744 young adults under twenty-three who quit school and are now in the labor force. There were almost equal numbers of both sexes. We questioned the gifted and the dull, the ambitious and the lazy, the bright-eyed scholar and the bewildered delinquent. The young people we questioned are an accurate cross-section from all regions of the nation, from all levels of family income, education and occupation.

In effect, we have created the typical or composite American youth, and while the facets of his character may fog or gleam, depending on the individual, we now know fairly well what he is as a group.

Here is what we've found:

No one can say that the American youth is going to hell. He's not. But he is a pampered hothouse plant and likes it that way. The beatnik [proto-hippies of the late 1950s and early 1960s] is a rarity, the delinquent is a minority.

Our typical youth will settle for low success rather than risk high failure. He has little spirit of adventure. He wants to marry early—at twenty-three or twenty-four—after a college education. He wants two or three children and a spouse who is "affectionate, sympathetic, considerate and moral"; rarely does he want a mate with intelligence, curiosity or ambition. He wants a little ranch house, an inexpensive new car, a job with a large company, and a chance to watch TV each evening after the smiling children are asleep in bed.

He is a reluctant patriot who expects nuclear war in his time and would rather compromise than risk an all-out war. He is highly religious yet winks at dishonesty. He wants very little because he has so much and is unwilling to risk what he has. Essentially he is quite conservative and cautious. He is old before his time; almost middle-aged in his teens.

While he has high respect for education, he is critical of it—as he is about religion—and he is abysmally ignorant of the economic system that has made him what he is and of the system that threatens it.

## Generation Nice

In general, the typical American youth shows few symptoms of frustration, and is most unlikely to rebel or involve himself in crusades of any kind. He likes himself the way he is, and he likes things as they are.

The United States has bred a generation of nice little boys and girls who are just what we have asked them to be and what we so frequently say they are not. They will one day shape the nation. And there are those who say the world will trample a gentle generation. As Leo Durocher has said, "Nice guys finish last."

Of course, the nation is endowed with [examples of] hardy, vigorous young people. . . . But they are scattered thinly through the land. We can think of the two smooth-cheeked Miami high-school boys who are coldly furious at the state of the nation: one is aiming for a United States Senate seat. the other won't settle for less than the White House. There is the twenty-one-year-old airline stewardess who learned to fly at sixteen and acts as "a sort of mother-confessor" to harried businessmen who are her passengers. We remember the young college boy who reads great gulps of history and economics and almost makes a vocation of writing letters to Congressmen. There is the calm high-school girl who "would like to help the world in some small way," and the Kansas college boy who has tithed since he was in the ninth grade "because I'm getting much more from life than I'm giving." These are exceptions.

We can also remember the typical: the whining boy in Albuquerque, a huge youth—six feet, three inches tall—who, in the last two years, has had three cars of his own and a motor scooter, who says he'd like to help the unemployed but won't, for he knows "they'd just want a thousand dollars or something." There is the Pennsylvania girl who says, "Any normal person will cheat in school. It's up to the teacher to stop it." And the college boy who wants a Navy career "so I can retire early" and the Texas youth who is "just dying to travel. But I've gotta go first class, of course." And the Los Angeles boy who stole a radio because he "just couldn't see mowing fifty lawns to earn it." We see a hundred well-scrubbed faces politely—and shamelessly—revealing compromise, conformity and intellectual poverty. We see them in their cotton-batting world of gossip, television thrillers and adolescent mating rites. These are the majority; this is the generation that will participate in the perpetuation—or the liquidation—of the human race.

Yet who can really judge a generation from its words? Youth has often said one thing and done another. Pacifism was a college-campus fad before Pearl Harbor; yet when the bombs fell and the nation was committed, youth responded admirably. Minds changed quickly. The nation, and its youth, rallied to a challenge. As then, we now have youth who have not yet caught fire, who have a kindling point. But where is the point on the scale of challenge? And how many can be kindled?

## Lacking Necessity

The serious young man in New Orleans hunched himself deeper into the living-room couch. "It may not be as hopeless as you think," he told us, "What my generation lacks is necessity." He pointed to us. "You didn't lack it. You had a war. You had a depression. I really think if we were faced with the necessity, we'd respond."

He swiveled himself on the cushion. "Look," he said. "We have neither the naïveté nor the urgency of our parents. They felt that they mattered; that they could do something about conditions. We feel that nothing we do will make any difference.

"You know," he said thoughtfully, "there are no individuals any more. There are no more Lindberghs flying the ocean alone, or real men with real names and real identities exploring the frozen north. It's all done by teamwork and helicopters and submarines backstopped by a thousand scientists and technicians. Even the astronauts are not people; they're a team." He paused. "And there's no longer any sense of shock. How can we be indignant, especially after knowing what we do about World War II and humanity?"

Few young Americans are so articulate or so perceptive. What the fatalistic young man of New Orleans is saying, in effect, is that many American youth have not yet joined the human race. Our statistics bear him out. Take their greatest fears and problems, for instance. Two thirds of them expect to see a nuclear war annihilating populations, but they do not fear it; they somehow feel immortal. There is no dominating specter overshadowing them. Only 14 per cent report nuclear war as their greatest fear; other fears are more immediate. Almost one fourth of the college men fear personal failure in life; about 15 per cent of the college girls fear social insecurity or not being loved. Youth's other fears are widely scattered. They include poverty or financial failure (3 per cent), unhappy marriage (2 per cent), death (12 per cent), and illness (4 per cent).

The most frequently reported "most serious problem of youth" is a loosely wrapped bundle of worries that they call "the future." For the most part, this is a package of personal irritants including job-finding, wife-hunting and nest-making. About one fifth of all the respondents mention these categories, with one third of the college students considering them important. Almost one fifth of the high-schoolers list "morals, drinking and sex," but only 10 per cent of the older youth report these as serious problems. Only 9 per cent name war, or world instability, as a problem, although the college group is twice as concerned as the average.

## Favoring Compromise over War

Jean Brown, a nineteen-year-old junior at the University of Kentucky, says, "Of course youth is concerned about the possibility of war. But for most of us war is a great big fairy tale told us by our parents. We don't believe it can happen to us." Yet the threat has had some impact. They rattle sabers cautiously.

We asked them: "If this country should become involved in another limited war, such as Korea, do you think we should try to end it on the basis of compromise, or should we fight it out even if this means getting into an all-out war?" Much like their parents a generation earlier, they answered: "Compromise." More than three fourths of the girls and almost 60 per cent of the boys say they would be unwilling to risk war: however, 44 per cent of the college males would refuse to compromise. Regionally, the West and Midwest are more willing to fight: Southern youth are most reluctant.

A Florida college girl told us, "Every step of our country was built on compromise; do we change the pattern now?" Her male classmate said, "To compromise doesn't mean we're soft, you know. And anyway, we have more to live for and more to lose. Therefore we're more willing to compromise to save it. I'd rather be alive than dead." Another boy said thoughtfully, "I don't know. For eight years now—for almost half our lives—we've been told that everything is peachy fine. Now we know it's not. Americans have been treated like children and denied the harsh truths. Now we're told to act, but we don't know what to do. I'm confused."

Adding to their confusions is a conviction that Communism is getting stronger, and that Russia will move ahead of the United States in many vital areas. Almost 50 per cent feel that Communism will strengthen its hold on the world during the next twenty-five years. About two thirds of our youth predict that the U.S.S.R. will surpass this nation someday in one way or another; almost 40 per cent say it will be superior in military power and space achievement, and although the college group feels slightly more secure in these two areas, it is also considerably concerned with reports of Soviet superiority in education, science, medicine and mathematics.

## Ignorance of Foreign Threats

These things they feel, and yet they say they do not fear them. They seem to be waiting for fate to overtake them, and behind their fatalism lies immense and startling ignorance. By their own testimony they do not understand either the Soviet Union or the United States. When asked to compare Soviet and American economies, almost 9 per cent said capitalism had no advantages over Communism; more than 40 per cent could name no advantages. Although college ignorance was less, almost one third of this group either could name no U.S. advantage (25 per cent) or said there was none (7 per cent).

In Albuquerque, blond, sixteen-year-old Linda Greene admits,

"I don't know enough about Communism to talk about it. Everybody says it's bad but we're never told what it is. I think the people who want us to be better teen-agers should tell us what Communism is." In San Francisco another sixteen-year-old, Marleen Hoff, a gentle, blue-eyed youngster, is equally bewildered. "Well," she says jerkily, trying to arrange her thoughts, "about American Communists—there aren't too many of them. But Communism means war, and therefore I fear Communism. I guess I don't really know too much about it. But they do seem stronger." Perhaps Linda and Marleen can be excused, at sixteen, for knowing little about a foreign nation's threats. But they are typical of most American youth. . . .

## Embracing Religion

It is not easy to be secure in a world of contradiction, disillusion and controversy, but our youth seem to have succeeded. In doing so, many of them have turned inward, speaking only to themselves, living portions of their lives without meaning or responsibility; and huge numbers have turned to religion. Eighty-four per cent of them are church members, and more than half attend church regularly.

Each Sunday in the chapel at Kirtland Air Force Base at Albuquerque, New Mexico, nineteen-year-old Richard P. Copeland teaches a sixth-grade Sunday-school class. "Cope" is a physics technician, an airman second class, a husky, happy, energetic youth who helps space scientists construct instrument packages which measure space radiation. Frequently, at the Los Alamos laboratories, he helps test a package before it is launched as high as 3500 miles. He often works from seven A.M. to midnight or later, and his labors are exciting. "Every hour, every day there's something different," he says. "I'm a man fighting the world, and I'm winning the battle." On weekdays he prepares to wage nuclear war in space; on Sunday he turns to God.

Like most American youth, Cope gets great comfort from religion. "The laws are there, and you can't go wrong with them," he says. "It gives you security; it gives life hope and meaning."

Cope has a strong feeling of social responsibility, "I won't be happy if I'm not benefiting man," he says, but his work does not bother his conscience. "I know that my work can contribute to great violence, but it can be used for good as well as for horrible destruction. Man will decide to use it as he sees fit." In one sense

Cope is buck-passing, divorcing himself from mankind, saying "Man" will decide, as if he were not a part of Man. In this respect he is fairly typical of American youth—and perhaps of America itself. For youth correctly blames others for the problems facing them and incorrectly says that others will solve the problems for them.

And Cope is typical in strong religious beliefs. Seventy-four per cent of our youth believe in God "very firmly": 76 per cent think of God as an omnipresent judge who observes all individual human actions and rewards or punishes them; 78 per cent believe in a hereafter; almost two thirds of the high-school and working youth believe the Bible is "completely true," and 22 per cent of our college youth believe every word of the Testaments. Nine per cent of the college boys and 5 per cent of the college girls say they don't believe in God, but nearly two thirds of our collegians are "very firm" believers.

Yet youth as a whole, while quite religious, is quite critical of the church as an institution. The girls, who are much more religious, have more criticism than the boys. The college group, which is least religious, is more critical than high-school and working youth; and youth in the South, the most religious region, are more critical than youth in less religious sections of the nation. Fifty-four per cent of the youth expressed dissatisfaction with religion, and their comments cut through all religious sects. The most frequent complaints are that the church fails to explain itself and its precepts, that it fails to stress its true meaning fervently enough, that it is not reaching the people, and that sermons are too vague and muddy. Many charge that "the church is not keeping pace with a changing world" and express disgust with what they call "too much ritual and mysticism.". . .

Youth spends little time reading because he's busy with other things—mainly with the opposite sex. The typical youth dates once a week, but college girls have twice as many dates as the typical American girl. At the high-school-sophomore level about half the boys and three fourths of the girls have started dating; by the time they are seniors 80 per cent are dating regularly, and only 10 per cent of the college youth say they do not date. They go to movies (about twice a month); they love to dance (89 per cent of the girls but only 75 per cent of the boys); watch television (about two hours a day); listen to the radio (about an hour a day); and talk. But in all these things they want a potential mate close by. To use their own term, they want to "couple-up."

Fifteen-year-old Eileen Trust of Philadelphia, a charming, vivacious brunette with a "bubble" coif, goes steady with a boy friend named Jay. She sees Jay daily, and every Friday evening he appears at her suburban home to take her out or spend the evening there. Each Saturday morning he reappears and "we go for walks, or he takes me to lunch, or we play records.". . .

Like most young people, Eileen and Jay are television addicts, preferring thrillers (Eileen calls them "horrors"), comedies and Westerns in that order. Why does she prefer thrillers? Because she likes them, she says quite simply. But Anthony J. Reiger Jr., a seventeen-year-old New Orleans youth, has a more perceptive answer. Anthony is a hard-working boy; last summer he rose each morning at two o'clock to deliver nearly 200 morning newspapers. He earns about twenty-five dollars a week, saving it for college. In a wistful sort of way he wants to travel. "I want to do it right," he says. "I don't want to go on a cattle boat or work my way around the world. I don't think I could stand those kind of men, who spit and curse and do bad things. I don't want to see the raws of life.". . .

## The Vigorous Minority

An essential ingredient of most of their activities is companionship; even their television watching involves joint staring with a companion nearby. Togetherness appeals; singleness does not. But not all of them, of course, need peer approval or togetherness as they live their lives. There is a vigorous minority—mostly college males—who do not hide from "the raws of life" and who want to shape a better world. Politics attracts them. In our sample, four young men stand out especially.

Energetic and indignant, leftish liberal in his politics, courageous and impatient, eighteen-year-old William Bancroft is a light-skinned San Francisco Negro. His father is an attorney, and Bill is going to study law. Already he is an active member of four political-action groups. Last summer he spent six weeks in New York City at a youth Encampment for Citizenship where he studied "economics, labor relations, agriculture, jazz, poetry and politics." Last April he marched with 200 other Californians in a fifty-five-mile "Peace Walk." His mayor, his governor and his President have received letters from him "because I want to have a home and a family and peace. And I want to make sure I get them."

Two young men 3000 miles away in Miami also want what Bill wants, but their views are somewhat different. Ralph Milone Jr. is seventeen; his close friend Roger Davis is sixteen. Both are vigorous, intelligent and calmly articulate; both are ultra-conservatives. They favor the impeachment of Chief Justice Earl Warren "because of his 92 per cent pro-Communist voting record." Roger calls the metropolitan government of Miami "a form of miniature Communism." They feel the nation would have few problems today if [conservative Republican] Barry Goldwater had been elected President years ago. Frequently their letters to the editor are published in Miami newspapers. They distribute John Birch [a right-wing political group] literature.

When he was fifteen, young Ralph organized and became president of the Republican Youth League of Dade County; Roger is its secretary. The forty-member group, aged fourteen to twenty-one, meets once a month to praise or condemn political acts or actors and to plan letter-writing campaigns to influence legislation.

Somewhere between these liberal-conservative extremes is twenty-year-old Allan Wicker of Independence, Kansas. Wicker is a college junior, a short, thoughtful, intelligent youth who is resolutely religious, but not evangelical. Since he was fifteen he has tithed to his church—"When I got a dollar for mowing a lawn, I put away a dime." Our questions about his tithing puzzled him. "Why, any balanced person knows that he gets more from life than he gives," he says. "In order to be happy, you have to give instead of take." Occasionally he teaches Sunday school to local college students.

Last summer he worked as a reporter on his hometown daily. Two summers ago, after months of unsuccessful letter-writing and some intricate maneuvering, he managed a job as a deck boy on a Swedish oil tanker. In Antwerp his shipmates showed him the town, and he saw some of the raws of life. He was unfazed. "I had never seen drunks or prostitutes before, but I wasn't shocked. These things exist." After a few weeks with a student tour, he spent the rest of the summer as a laborer on a German farm. Now at the University of Kansas, Allan is preparing for a career with the State Department.

## Little Interest in Politics

The typical American youth, however, is quite willing to let Bill Bancroft or the Miami conservatives or Allan Wicker dominate the nation's policies, eighty-three per cent of our young people have no intention of entering politics. Many describe it as a "dirty, selfish, narrow, compromising game." And a peace walk—for all their hopes for peace—would either bore or embarrass them. Only one third—nearly half the high-school boys—want to vote at age eighteen, and these quote the cliché: "Old enough to fight; old enough to vote." Those opposed admit they are "too immature" or uninformed.

They have a simple mental picture of the two political parties. Republicans are "rich men opposing change and bound by the past" who have good manners and are socially acceptable. Democrats are "progressive common men agreeable to change" who are uncouth; one youth calls them "loud-mouth, like Harry Truman." The college group, however, equates Democrats with intellectuals, the Republicans with wealth and materialism. However, 45 per cent of American youth admit they have no image of either party.

With the exception of a small number of college youth (30 per cent of the males; 19 per cent of the females), our young people reflect the political values of their parents. If they had voted in the last election, Nixon would have carried the colleges with 51 per cent of the vote; Kennedy would have taken 55 per cent of the high-school vote and 58 per cent of the working youth's vote. Those few who have broken with their parents' political patterns say they are "more flexible, more independent and more liberal" than their parents.

And perhaps it will distress Miami's Republican Youth League—as well as Barry Goldwater—to learn that as of now, there is no conservative surge in U.S. colleges, or anywhere else among American youth. In American colleges Nelson Rockefeller is four times as popular, and Richard Nixon is three times as popular, as Barry Goldwater; in high school and among the working youth Nixon and Rockefeller reverse their positions, but Goldwater remains a poor third. In all groups he attracts only one eighth of American youth.

Like Allan Wicker, slightly more than half of our youth say they have given "much thought" to making this a better world, but unlike Wicker, they plan to improve it by improving themselves. They tell us that reform can come if "I inform myself," or "understand others." Someone else, somewhere else, can do the hard work and the hard thinking that is needed. Yet Wicker has some companionship in his desire for foreign service—as long as hardship is eliminated. Forty per cent of our youth say they are interested in the Peace Corps, but almost half of these would like to serve with the corps in Western Europe. A few mention Paris as a desirable post. About 8 per cent are interested in Latin America; similar numbers would like to serve in the Far East or Africa.

And how does the new generation feel about school integration in the South? Except for Southern youth, two thirds of them approve. But Southern youth, incredibly, seem to have a stronger feeling against Negroes in the classroom than Negroes next door, while the remainder of the nation's youth object more to Negro neighbors than to Negro classmates. Here's what they said of their racial feelings:

|  | *White Southern Youth* | *White Youth in Rest of Nation* |
|---|---|---|
| Should Integration Be Required in Southern Public Schools? | 22% Yes | 65% Yes |
| Would You Object to a Majority of Negroes in Your Class? | 27  No | 64  No |
| Would You Object to a Negro Family Next Door? | 30  No | 58  No |

## Close to the Nest

The younger generation's attitude toward parents, although tinged with condescension at times, may surprise older folks pleasantly.

"When I was fourteen," Mark Twain once confided to the world, "my father was so ignorant I could hardly stand to have him around. But when I got to be twenty-one, I was astonished at how much the old man had learned in seven years."

In this respect American youth has hardly changed since Mark Twain was a boy. Only recently a New Hampshire boy told us, "When you're sixteen, you wish your parents would dry up and blow away. But when you're eighteen, you find they're fun, and you like to show them off. I know a girl who is embarrassed when her father jumps over the porch railing to greet her boy friend. Listen, when she's my age, she'll be proud he can still do it."

Actually American youngsters are fairly close to their parents.

When they need advice, nearly 70 per cent of them turn first to their parents; and nearly a third do not plan to rear their children any differently from the way they were reared. . . .

Yet parents in many ways have never been more generous. Their generosity in financial matters may have affected our youth curiously.

The nation has produced a generation of stay-at-homes and conservative spenders. We asked them: "If someone gave you $5000, what would you do with it?" Three fourths of them replied: "Put it in the bank," although a third of these planned to withdraw it for education. About 15 per cent of the boys would spend some of it for an automobile, and about one fourth of the girls would give all or part of it to church, charity or the family. But except for college women, there was hardly any mention of travel; and less than 2 percent would use it to go into business for themselves. In fact, American youth is not much interested in being self-employed. Almost two thirds would rather work for a large corporation than start their own small company.

But while they seek security in the corporation, they want independence from government. Almost 70 per cent told us that they preferred to work out their own economic problems rather than have the government maintain a minimum living standard for all. The girls are slightly more interested in a welfare state; but 80 percent of the college boys rejected it. Concerning labor unions, the more independent college group is also more disapproving of the closed shop; while about two thirds of high-school and working youth disapprove, 78 per cent of the collegians were opposed. However, only one third of American youth disapprove of labor unions. The girls are slightly more approving of the labor movement, and there is slightly less approval among the college and the working youth.

## Roots of Apathy

How did youth become so bland? So cautious? So self-satisfied, secure and unambitious? And are they really so much different from the youth of yesterday? Memories are unreliable for comparing this generation with the last; yet memories are all we have. Unfortunately this study of American youth is not a repeat of one done twenty years ago, and therefore we cannot compare with accuracy. But our youth themselves point out that they are different from their parents, and they don't hestitate to tell us why.

In Seattle, Bryce G. Horst says, "Our parents led a tougher life—they fought a depression and a war. And they've protected us. They've made sure that we have more than they had. We're pampered." An Eastern college girl says simply, "Of course we're soft. We got too much too soon. There isn't much we want that our parents don't give us." And the director of admissions at a large university says, "Parents have done just about everything they could to destroy character in their children. If student cars were banned on campus, I think parents would help their off-spring violate the rule." A California high-schooler says, "Goals? We've got no goals. Our parents have achieved them all for us."

Certainly parents must share the blame. Denied so much when capitalism seemed to totter thirty years ago, they have been bountiful with their children. And some must wonder now if capitalism might not be destroying itself with its own success. The largess of the father has weakened the son.

But there are other contributing factors. The world is constantly confronted with overwhelming crises—Berlin, Laos, Cuba, Algeria, Tunisia, the Congo, South Vietnam—and our youth unhardened in the crucible of struggle, might well turn inward to escape responsibility.

Allan Wicker says, "We've got to teach our children to think, and you don't do this in front of TV. We have to make them excited about ideas. And we've got to convince them that there's nothing shameful in being different. I don't mean they should be different just to attract attention, but they should know that every great person is different; that you can't do extraordinary things and be like everybody else."

How many of our youth will want to be—or can be—extraordinary? In an extraordinary age how will they react when tested? Will they do as well as their fathers did under the pressures of war and economic slump? A college girl says they will. "All we need is motive; then you'll see."

But the older generation wonders. In the meantime American parents candidly admit they are spoiling and pampering this new generation. They admit it, cluck their tongues and keep on pampering.

# CHRONOLOGY

**January 3:** President Dwight D. Eisenhower severs diplomatic relations with Cuba after Communist dictator Fidel Castro nationalizes U.S. businesses and forges an alliance with the Soviet Union.

**January 16:** Two black students, Charlayne Hunter and Hamilton Holmes, reenter the University of Georgia in Athens following a federal court order overturning their suspension by a segregationist school board. The students are the first blacks to attend the university.

**January 20:** John F. Kennedy is inaugurated the thirty-fifth president of the United States in Washington, D.C. His inaugural address expresses a strong commitment to defeating the spread of communism.

**January 28:** President Kennedy approves the Counterinsurgency Plan (CIP) for Vietnam, which serves as the basis for expanded U.S. military assistance to South Vietnamese troops.

**January 30:** In his first State of the Union address, President Kennedy describes his proposals for increased defense spending and an economic program to lift the country out of recession.

**January 31:** The U.S. Mercury space program launches a capsule carrying Ham, a chimpanzee, on a successful suborbital spaceflight.

**February 12:** The Soviet Union launches a satellite into orbit that will operate as a firing platform for the *Venus I* space probe developed to explore the planet Venus.

**March 1:** President Kennedy signs an executive order establishing the Peace Corps and announces that the new organization will recruit young volunteers with specialized skills to work in developing nations.

**March 21:** The United States, Britain, and the Soviet Union meet in Geneva, Switzerland, for talks on banning nuclear weapons testing. Soviet proposals for creating a weapons control board are rejected.

**March 23:** President Kennedy announces his desire for a peace settlement in the Southeast Asian nation of Laos, where Soviet-backed Communists are fighting U.S.-supported forces.

**March 25:** The *Explorer X* satellite is launched by the United States. On the same day, the Soviet Union launches a space capsule with a dog on board, marking their final rehearsal for a manned spaceflight.

**March 27:** At a meeting of the Southeast Asia Treaty Organization (SEATO) in Bangkok, Thailand, the U.S. secretary of state, Dean Rusk, announces that democratic nations must defend the region against Communist insurgents.

**March 31:** Warsaw Pact nations—the Soviet Union and its Communist allies—meet in Moscow and describe West Germany as a "hotbed of war danger." They demand that the United States, France, and Britain broker a peace treaty between East and West Germany.

**April 6:** Demonstrators protesting a ban on folk music performances in New York's Washington Square Park scuffle with police, leading to several arrests.

**April 12:** Soviet astronaut Yuri A. Gagarin completes the first-ever manned spaceflight after orbiting the earth for 108 minutes aboard the *Vostok I* space capsule.

**April 17:** President Kennedy orders a brigade of Cuban exiles, trained and recruited by the U.S. Central Intelligence Agency, to invade Cuba at the Bay of Pigs. Planned with the intention of instigating a popular uprising against Communist dictator Fidel Castro, the covert operation is a complete failure.

**May 1:** A commercial airliner en route from Miami to Key West, Florida, is hijacked by Puerto Rican–born Abntulio Ramirez Ortiz and forced to land in Havana, Cuba.

**May 5:** Navy commander Alan B. Shepard becomes the first U.S. astronaut to enter space after he completes a fifteen-minute suborbital flight aboard the Mercury space program's *Freedom 7* capsule; President Kennedy signs legislation raising the minimum wage to $1.25 by 1963.

**May 9–15:** Vice President Lyndon B. Johnson travels to Southeast Asia to assure leaders there that despite the situation in Laos, the United States can be counted on to support their struggles against communism.

**May 14:** Civil rights Freedom Riders traveling the South to protest racial segregation in public buses and bus stations are attacked by white mobs in two Alabama cities.

**May 20–21:** Racial violence continues against the Freedom Riders in Montgomery, Alabama, after Attorney General Robert Kennedy is assured by Alabama authorities that the protesters will be protected.

**May 25:** President Kennedy delivers his second State of the Union address, asking Congress to allocate more funds for the space program and the military.

**June 3–4:** President Kennedy and Soviet premier Nikita S. Khrushchev meet at the Vienna Summit, in Vienna, Austria, in an attempt to resolve disputes over the control of West Berlin, the war in Laos, Soviet support for Cuba, and nuclear weapons testing. The president describes the talks as "somber," and leaves without securing any concessions from Khrushchev.

**June 15:** Khrushchev announces that the Soviet Union will spurn any U.S. attempt to limit its rights of access to West Berlin.

**July 2:** Renowned American author Ernest Hemingway dies of a self-inflicted gunshot wound at his home in Ketchum, Idaho.

**July 25:** In a speech to the American people on the Berlin crisis, President Kennedy announces that U.S. forces are readying for war against an unyielding Soviet Union. He also warns that nuclear conflict is a possibility.

**August 6–7:** Soviet astronaut Gherman S. Titov orbits the earth seventeen times in a twenty-five-hour flight—the most prolonged manned spaceflight to date.

**August 13:** The Soviet Union orders its East German puppet regime to close the border between East and West Berlin, halting the flow of people from the Communist East to the democratic West. Days later, East German troops begin construction on the Berlin Wall.

**August 31:** The Soviet Union announces that it will resume the atmospheric testing of nuclear weapons.

**September 5:** President Kennedy announces that the United States will resume the underground testing of nuclear weapons in Nevada.

**October 9:** The New York Yankees defeat the Cincinnati Reds to win the 1961 World Series.

**October 17:** Premier Khrushchev proposes to delay the year-end deadline he had imposed on negotiating a peace settlement between East and West Germany.

**November 3:** General Maxwell D. Taylor releases a report to the president warning that U.S. interests are at stake in South Vietnam and that prompt U.S. military and economic action could help the South Vietnamese defeat the Vietcong.

**November 11:** Secretary of State Rusk and Secretary of Defense Robert S. McNamara deliver a top-secret memorandum to the president advising that the United States commit itself to preventing the fall of South Vietnam to communism. They state that the involvement of U.S. combat troops may become necessary in the near future.

**November 29:** The U.S. space program launches a capsule with a chimpanzee on board, which orbits the earth twice in a three-hour flight.

**December:** The U.S. Department of Defense releases the report *Fallout Protection: What to Know and Do About Nuclear Attack;* a new dance craze called "the Twist," inspired by a Chubby Checker song by the same name, captures the nation's fancy.

**December 2:** In a televised address from Havana, Cuba, Fidel Castro describes himself as a "Marxist-Leninist" who will lead Cuba into communism.

**December 16:** Civil rights leader Martin Luther King Jr. and 264 blacks are arrested in Albany, Georgia, for protesting the arrest of blacks jailed after a demonstration outside the courthouse where eleven Freedom Riders stand trial for disturbing the peace.

# FOR FURTHER RESEARCH

## The Berlin Crisis

John P.S. Gearson and Kori N. Schake, *The Berlin Wall Crisis: Perspectives on Cold War Alliances*. New York: Palgrave Macmillan, 2002.

Fred Kaplan, "JFK's First Strike Plan," *Atlantic Monthly*, October 2001.

John F. Kennedy, "Berlin Crisis; Address, July 25, 1961," *Vital Speeches*, August 15, 1961.

*Life*, "Wall That Divides the World," September 8, 1961.

David E. Murphy, *Battleground Berlin: CIA vs. KGB in the Cold War*. New Haven, CT: Yale University Press, 1997.

*Nation*, "Berlin: Background to Crisis, with Editorial Comments," July 15, 1961.

Eloise Schindler, *A Mighty Fortress Was the Berlin Wall*. Philadelphia: Xlibris, 2002.

Mike Sewell, *The Cold War*. New York: Cambridge University Press, 2002.

## Cuba and the Bay of Pigs Invasion

James G. Blight and Peter Kornbluh, eds., *Politics of Illusion: The Bay of Pigs Invasion Reexamined*. Boulder, CO: Lynne Rienner, 1998.

Peter Kornbluh, ed., *Bay of Pigs Declassified: The Secret CIA Report on the Invasion of Cuba*. New York: New, 1998.

Walter LaFeber, "The Unlearned Lessons—Lest We Forget the Bay of Pigs," *Nation*, April 19, 1986.

Grayston L. Lynch, *Decision for Disaster: Betrayal at the Bay of Pigs*. Dulles, VA: Brassey's, 2000.

*New Republic*, "What Went Wrong?" May 1, 1961.

Juan C. Rodriguez, *Bay of Pigs and the CIA*. New York: Ocean, 1999.

Victor Andres Triay, *Bay of Pigs: An Oral History of Brigade 2506*. Gainesville: University Press of Florida, 2001.

## Fallout Shelters

Norman Cousins, "Shelters, Survival, and Common Sense," *Saturday Review*, October 28, 1961.

Department of Defense, Office of Civil Defense, *Fallout Protection: What to Know and Do About Nuclear Attack*. Washington, DC: Government Printing Office, 1961.

*Life*, "Fallout Shelters," September 15, 1961.

Walton W. McCarthy, *The Nuclear Shelterist*. Great Neck, NY: Todd & Honeywell, 1985.

*Nation*, "Shelter Racket," September 23, 1961.

James Reston, "How to Be Evaporated in Style," *New York Times*, October 15, 1961.

———, "Kennedy's Shelter Policy Reexamined," *New York Times*, November 26, 1961.

Kenneth D. Rose, *One Nation, Underground: A History of the Fallout Shelter*. New York: New York University Press, 2001.

## The Freedom Riders and the Civil Rights Movement

Charlotte Devree, "The Young Negro Rebels," *Harper's*, October 1961.

E.F. Goldman, "Progress: By Moderation and Agitation," *New York Times Magazine*, June 18, 1961.

G.W. Johnson, "Who Turned the Bull Loose?" *New Republic*, June 5, 1961.

David Niven, *The Politics of Injustice: The Kennedys, The Freedom Rides, and the Electoral Consequences of a Moral Compromise*. Knoxville: University of Tennessee Press, 2003.

William Rorabaugh, *Kennedy and the Promise of the Sixties*. New York: Cambridge University Press, 2002.

*Time*, "Trouble in Alabama; Freedom Riders," May 26, 1961.

*U.S. News & World Report*, "Untold Story of the 'Freedom Rides,'" October 23, 1961.

## Music and the Arts

Nelson Algren, "Hemingway: The Dye That Did Not Run," *Nation*, November 18, 1961.

Gene Bluestein, "Songs of the Silent Generation," *New Republic*, March 13, 1961.

Charles A. Brady, "Portrait of Hemingway," *America*, July 22, 1961.

David Hajdu, *Positively Fourth Street: The Lives and Times of Joan Baez, Bob Dylan, Mimi Baez Farina, and Richard Farina*. New York: Farrar, Straus & Giroux, 2002.

Jan Kindler, "Cops, 'Beatniks,' and Facts," *Village Voice*, April 13, 1961.

Alan Lomax, *Alan Lomax: Selected Writings, 1934–1995*. New York: Routledge, 2003.

*Newsweek*, "Hoots and Hollers on the Campus," November 27, 1961.

Tim A. Ross, "Rise and Fall of the Beats," *Nation*, May 27, 1961.

Pete Seeger, *Where Have All the Flowers Gone?: A Musical Autobiography*. Bethlehem, PA: Sing Out!, 1997.

Ruth Crawford Seeger and Judith Tick, *Music of American Folk Song*. Rochester, NY: University of Rochester Press, 2001.

*Time*, "Foggy Faggy Don't: Folk Singers of Greenwich Village," April 21, 1961.

Richie Unterberger, *Turn! Turn! Turn! The '60s Folk-Rock Revolution*. San Francisco: Backbeat Books, 2002.

## The Peace Corps

Raoul M. Barlow, "Paying the Price for Peace," *America*, April 8, 1961.

Benjamin DeMott, "The Peace Corps' Secret Mission," *Harper's*, September 1961.

Fritz Fischer, *Making Them Like Us: Peace Corps Volunteers in the 1960s*. Washington, DC: Smithsonian Institution, 2000.

Elizabeth Cobbs Hoffman, *All You Need Is Love: The Peace Corps and the Spirit of the 1960s*. Cambridge, MA: Harvard University Press, 2000.

George H.T. Kimble, "Challenges to the Peace Corps," *New York Times Magazine*, May 14, 1961.

Karen Schwarz, *What You Can Do for Your Country: Inside the Peace Corps—A Thirty Year History*. New York: Doubleday, 1993.

## Space Exploration

Martin J. Collins, *Space Race: The U.S.-U.S.S.R. Competition to Reach the Moon*. Rohnert Park, CA: Pomegranate Communications, 1999.

Anne Garton, *The Space Race*. New York: Cambridge University Press, 2002.

*Life*, "Shepard and USA Feel AOK," May 12, 1961.

Asif A. Siddiqi, *The Soviet Space Race with Apollo*. Gainesville: University Press of Florida, 2003.

*Time*, "Freedom's Flight," May 12, 1961.

*U.S. News & World Report*, "After Letdowns, Lift: First American in Space," May 15, 1961.

Patrick J. Walsh, *Echoes Among the Stars: A Short History of the U.S. Space Program*. Armonk, NY: M.E. Sharpe, 2000.

## The Student Movement

Philip G. Altbach, *Student Politics in America: A Historical Analysis*. Piscataway, NJ: Transaction, 1997.

Robert Cohen and Reginald E. Zelnik, eds., *The Free Speech Movement: Reflections on Berkeley in the 1960s*. Berkeley and Los Angeles: University of California Press, 2002.

Gerard J. DeGroot, *Student Protest.* Boston: Addison Wesley Longman, 1998.

Martin Luther King Jr., "Time for Freedom Has Come," *New York Times Magazine*, September 10, 1961.

Philip Rieff, "The Mirage of College Politics," *Harper's*, October 1961.

## The Vienna Summit

*Department of State Bulletin*, "Meetings at Vienna and London," June 26, 1961.

Lawrence Freedman, *Kennedy's Wars: Berlin, Cuba, Laos, and Vietnam.* New York: Oxford University Press, 2002.

*Newsweek*, "Personal Diplomacy," June 12, 1961.

*New Yorker*, "Letter from Washington," June 3, 1961.

Marta Randall and Arthur M. Schlesinger Jr., *John F. Kennedy.* New York: Chelsea House, 1989.

*U.S. News & World Report*, "Khrushchev's Report on Vienna Conference," June 26, 1961.

## Vietnam

Loren Baritz, *Backfire: A History of How American Culture Led Us into Vietnam and Made Us Fight the Way We Did.* Baltimore: Johns Hopkins University Press, 1998.

John Galloway, *The Kennedys and Vietnam.* New York: Facts On File, 1971.

David E. Kaiser, *American Tragedy: Kennedy, Johnson, and the Origins of the Vietnam War.* Cambridge, MA: Harvard University Press, 2001.

A.J. Langguth, *Our Vietnam: 1954–1975.* New York: Simon & Schuster, 2000.

Robert Hopkins Miller, *Vietnam and Beyond: A Diplomat's Cold War Education.* Lubbock: Texas Tech University Press, 2002.

Neil Sheehan et al., *The Pentagon Papers as Published by the* New York Times. New York: Quadrangle Books, 1971.

Richard H. Shultz Jr., *The Secret War Against Hanoi: Kennedy's and Johnson's Use of Spies, Saboteurs, and Covert Warriors in North Vietnam.* New York: HarperCollins, 1999.

## Websites

Black History Quest, http://blackquest.com. The Black History Quest website offers a wealth of information on the struggle for African American civil rights during the late 1950s and 1960s. Resources include articles profiling African Americans of historical distinction, time lines, and photographs.

Close Up Foundation, www.closeup.org. The foundation offers papers, articles, and time lines on the subject of U.S.-Cuban relations, including in-depth coverage of the Bay of Pigs invasion and the Cuban missile crisis.

The Free Speech Movement Archives, www.fsm-a.org. This website covers the student free speech and protest movements that began at the University of California at Berkeley in the early 1960s. The archives include photographs, personal anecdotes, and scholarly analyses.

The John F. Kennedy Library and Museum, www.cs.umb.edu/jfklibrary. The John F. Kennedy Library and Museum, located in Boston, Massachusetts, maintains a website offering access to speeches, sound files, photographs, and other online resources documenting the presidency of John F. Kennedy.

The National Aeronautics and Space Administration (NASA) History Office, www.hq.nasa.gov. This NASA website presents the history of the U.S. space program through documents, photographs, and other archival materials.

The Sixties Project, http://lists.village.virginia.edu/sixties. This website provides links to discussion papers, journals, scholarships, and personal anecdotes of the major events of the 1960s.

# INDEX